PSYCHOLOGY IN THE FI-NANCIAL MARKETS

MASTERING THE MENTAL GAME OF INVESTING TO MANAGE RISK, CULTIVATE CALM, AND ACCUMU-LATE LONG-TERM WEALTH

RILEY WHITMAN

Copyright © 2025 BY SYNAST PUBLISHING

Published by SYNAST PUBLISHING

All rights reserved.

ISBN: 978-1-968418-37-3

INTRODUCTION

In the high-stakes arena of financial markets, where fortunes can be made or lost in the blink of an eye, understanding the psychological dynamics at play is as critical as mastering the technical aspects of trading. This book delves into the often-overlooked mental game of investing, a facet that can significantly influence outcomes in both turbulent and stable market conditions. By focusing on the psychological forces that subtly guide investment decisions, it offers readers a comprehensive toolkit to navigate the emotional highs and lows inherent in the financial world.

The book begins by exploring the invisible psychological forces that drive financial decisions, illustrating how even the most seasoned investors can fall prey to emotional biases. Through the lens of recent high-profile financial events, such as the Archegos Capital implosion and the 2021 tech bubble, it deconstructs the myth of rational investing. These case studies serve as poignant reminders of how knowledge and action often diverge under emotional pressure.

Readers are invited to embark on a self-diagnostic journey, mapping their market mindset. This introspective process is designed to reveal inherent psychological tendencies, such as impulsivity or overconfidence, that could undermine investment success. The book provides practical exercises and quizzes to aid in this self-discovery, helping investors identify whether they are risk-takers or worriers, and aligning these insights with common investor archetypes.

In addition to self-assessment, the book offers strategies for mastering emotional regulation and developing resilience in the face of market volatility. It introduces mindfulness and cognitive behavioral techniques tailored for the fast-paced trading environment, empowering investors to maintain composure and make informed decisions even when market conditions are less than favorable.

Furthermore, the book advocates for the integration of psychological insights into everyday investing practices, emphasizing the concept of "Behavioral Alpha"—the competitive advantage gained by those who master their mental game. Through a blend of research-backed theories and real-world anecdotes, it demonstrates how psychological discipline can lead to outsized returns, surpassing technical acumen alone.

Ultimately, **"Psychology in the Financial Markets"** is not just a guide to managing risk and cultivating calm. It is also a call to action for investors to transform their mindset, paving the way for sustained wealth accumulation and a more profound understanding of the markets they navigate.

Table of Contents

Chapter 01: Introduction to Market Psychology

Understanding the Mind of the Market

The complex world of financial markets is vast and full of intrigues, and as such, in the world, the mind of the market has been equated to solving a complex code that determines the actions of droves of market players. This system is not only run by figures and facts but rather by the psychology of its participants. It is an ever-changing world with decisions being made, trades being taken, and trends evolving on the basis of an infinity of psychological considerations that at other times are being taken care of behind the scenes.

Psychology is central to the financial markets in that it influences the decisions of both individual investors and institutions. The centre of market psychology is the sentiment concept, which may be interpreted to mean the general mood that investors have towards a specific market or asset. This mood changes quickly and depends on the news, events, and psychological prejudices of each investor. On positive sentiment, there is a likelihood of the markets increasing due to this optimism and confidence. On the other hand, sentiment is often negative, which is why fear and uncertainty can cause sharp declines.

The herd mentality and the tendency of investors to follow the crowd regardless of the analysis or instincts are two of the most important psychological occurrences in the markets. Such a tendency is based on the human need to obey norms, as well as the fear of not receiving the profits that can be brought about. This may create bubbles during the boom periods in the market, where the prices of assets increase far above the actual prices, based on their values. On the other hand, when the market crashes, the same mob psychology can additionally contribute to the intensified crash since the herd gets scared, and people who hold or drive the stock start to sell alarmingly.

Another factor that contributes a lot to the nature of the market is cognitive biases. Confirmation bias, for example, makes investors search for information that justifies their already held beliefs and neglects other information that contradicts their beliefs. This may lead to overconfidence and bad decision-making because investors get blinded by observing the possible risks. The bias that can also cause incorrect perception and the basis of investment is the anchoring bias, where the investors become preoccupied with certain price levels or previous data that can limit their market positioning.

The cause of the market movements is strong emotions like fear and greed. Investor emotion can influence behaviors, where greed can make an investor take unreasonable risks during bull markets and where fear can encourage a panic-selling behavior during downturns. Market volatility tends to multiply these emotions to initiate a feedback loop that has the potential to result in extreme market conditions.

Investors should develop a level of self-awareness and emotional control that is rather high in order to negotiate the psychological peculiarities of the market successfully. It is important to be aware of mental patterns and prejudices that must be in operation to make rational investment decisions. The effects of emotional and psychological forces on investment portfolios can be lessened by adopting a restrained manner and thinking in long-term objectives instead of being bothered by short-term market fluctuations.

Finally, the market mind can be treated as the common psychology of market players. With this knowledge on the forces of psychology, investors are in a better position to make sound judgments and develop some predictability of market trends. This is demanding not just in learning economic and financial issues, but also in human factors that make up market forces. By so doing, this means that as much as one should learn the technicalities of investing, he or she should equally learn the psychology of the market.

Role of Emotions in Trading Decisions

Not only do numbers, charts, and figures of financial markets dominate in this complex world, but human emotions also play a huge part in it. The emotions are decisive in decision-making when it comes to trading, and they may forcefully smack down logic and reason. Fear, greed, and anxiety are some of the emotions that could significantly affect decision-making under the pressured conditions of trading, resulting in successes and catastrophes.

Fear is one of the strongest emotions in trading and can freeze investors and make them take irrational decisions. It can tend to occur during market drops, wherein the fear of losing money or losing possible gains can cause investors to liquidate investments at the first notice of the downturn, locking in the loss that could otherwise come later. This is a fear that may not only be applicable to newbie investors; even experienced traders could succumb to panic selling due to the fact that the instinctual fight-or-flight response sets in when markets are turbulent, thus clouding judgment.

On the contrary, greed might push the investors to take unnecessary risks and follow the lure of easy gains. The possibility of high returns may result in excessive leveraging of positions or spending in unstudied assets. The recent success of other traders can, in many cases, support this activity based on greed and create a sense of herding as people end up buying stocks or cryptocurrencies with excessive hype, only to risk large losses once the market normalizes.

Fear, another emotion that is common in trading, can be the cause of indecisiveness and lost opportunities. Market data and news flow continuously, and therefore, traders can easily get overwhelmed, such that the strategy they employ is questioned; this makes them hesitate to take their trades. Such hesitation may lead to lost opportunities for beneficial trades or being too late to make a position before the best time is lost.

Conversely, emotions may also be utilized positively in trading. The decision-making processes can be improved by enhancing emotional intelligence (recognition and control of one's emotions). Your self-awareness and ability to regulate your emotions allow you to face market psychology better. Traders should recognize emotions and acknowledge their existence without allowing them to influence steps in the market. This way, traders are able to conduct proper market analysis in a sound state of mind and make credible decisions.

In addition, feelings can be useful market sentiment indicators. The mood in the market can also be understood to give indications of market strengths and weaknesses that may be experienced. As an example, when fear is dominant, it can be a buying opportunity when prices are abnormally low, and excessive greed can herald a market correction.

People must develop skills to deal with emotions when trading. Mindfulness and cognitive behavioral strategies are some of the techniques that can assist traders in making unnecessary decisions and keep an even-handed demeanor. The exercise of the predetermined entry and exit strategies, together with acting in accordance with a strict trading strategy, should reduce the role of emotions.

To summarize, although emotions are part and parcel of human nature and trading, they may be countered when making trading decisions with a proper attitude and tactics. Through recognition and realization of the role of feelings, traders can easily negotiate through the financial markets and use the challenges that are presented as a stepping stone to growth and prosperity.

Psychological Traps in Investing

Psychological traps in the world of investing are an elusive villain that comes up when decisions need to be made in a hurry and with only partial information available. These pitfalls are essentially cognitive biases and emotions, and may considerably undermine even the well-thought-out investment plans. The pitfalls of overconfidence, loss aversion, anchoring, and confirmation bias are among the most common psychological pitfalls.

The overconfidence issue is a common trait in the minds of investors who become strong when they translate success to their dexterity without considering any external influence or the aspect of luck. Such bias is likely to result in excessive risk-taking, in the belief that investors have better insight or acumen. In bull runs, it is possible to get the illusion of control and overestimate one's capabilities, and this may give rise to bloated portfolios that are susceptible to abrupt declines.

Another Colander is a loss aversion in which a person feels the agony of losses more keenly than the delight of such gains. This bias may make the investors stay in the losing position too long, hoping it will come back, or sell off the winning stocks too early, in fear of losing an unachievable profit. Such action not only impacts the individual positions but also the entire performance of a portfolio, resulting in poor decision-making.

The concept of anchoring is that people depend on a certain reference point or initial information when making decisions. When investing, it more commonly presents as an overemphasis on a purchase price or prior market high that distorts judgment and leads to either a squandered opportunity or an added risk. As another example, an investor may be reluctant to sell a stock that has fallen below the purchase price, in the hope that it can 'get back to even', instead of looking at current and potential earnings of the investment as they actually are.

Confirmation bias refers to the propensity to seek information, interpret it in a way that happens to confirm one's preconception, and recall information in a way that suits preconceptions. This bias may be increased in the digital era, when bombarded with information, investors may become more susceptible to it. Investors can be deep in the echo chambers where they are consuming information and opinions and hearing what they want to hear without considering mixed evidence. This selective exposure may cause a one-sided understanding of the situation in the market and insufficient investment decisions.

The main coping mechanism to avoid these psychological traps is to be aware of oneself and disciplined. Structured decision procedures (e.g., pre-trade checklists and post-trade reviews) have the potential to aid in instilling a degree of objectivity. Another way to overcome the influence of confirmation bias is to question individual investment theses and solicit various opinions constantly.

Moreover, the ability to make decisions under stress can be escalated using emotional regulation strategies like mindfulness and stress management practices. The investors ought to also formulate good purchasing and selling rules that are not emotional but founded on objective standards. By being aware of these mental pitfalls and managing them, investors can become more resilient and advance their long-term investment performance.

Building a Psychological Edge

In high-stakes financial markets, where a psychological advantage may spell the difference between success and failure, learning how to develop such an edge can be a crucial step to success. The psychological aspect of investing can be one of the shadowy factors that influence the decisions and results. This chapter goes into the art of creating a psychological edge and provides a deep insight into how one can refine their mental constructs in order to traverse the rough seas of the market trends.

Emotional regulation is the heart of developing a psychological advantage. Investors often get swept away with emotions, the thrilling highs of the market climbs, to the ending lows of dips. It is not an inborn skill to be able to behave composure under such extremes, but one that can be developed by trying to learn to do so with intent. Good strategies are mindfulness and competent mental reframing, which can be used as effective techniques allowing investors to move beyond the emotional impulse and into more rational decision-making.

Mindfulness specifically gives a methodological system of settling the mind and concentrating. Quick-and-easy activities, such as the so-called 60-second market breath exercise, can be performed easily as part of the daily regimen, giving the trader a few moments to refresh when facing stressful situations in the market quickly. Through mindfulness, the impact of anxiety and fear can be reduced since the investor is focused on the present, and this leads to clarity of mind that is required when making a decision.

In addition to emotional control, getting a psychological advantage means forming consciousness about cognitive biases. Although such mental shortcuts are helpful in day-to-day life, they may cause severe judgment errors in the high-profile world of finances. It is also important to identify and curb these biases: overconfidence, loss aversion, and recency bias. It is recommended that investors conduct frequent bias audits, where the principal individuals can reflect on their mode of decision-making and attempt to find other sources of perspective to question their assumptions.

An applied component of developing a psychological advantage is developing sound decision-making models. Pre-trade checklists, as an equivalent structure, are used to make all decisions based on emotional sanity and analytical soundness. Such checklists cause investors to stop and reassess what might be driving them, making sure they are not acting on market noise rather than acting in the best interests of long-term objectives.

The learning capacity is another aspect that forms part of the foundation of psychological resilience. Reflections can be done after a trade. In these moments, the maker can analyze the decisions made on the previous trade both emotionally and analytically and get valuable information to be used in future decision-making. Using a reflective journal, the investors are in a position to record their emotional status, the reasons or rationale behind their decision, and the outcome of the same in a continuous chain of progress.

The real building of psychological edge is the state of mind on how to be assimilable and to develop permanently. It demands an approach that accepts it is a lifelong learning and self-assessment journey, as the psychology of investing is a moving landscape just as fluid as the market itself. Through these principles, investors may be able to turn psychological obstacles into opportunities to grow and develop a mental toolkit that can not only resist the burdens of the market but also use it as a means to continue success in the long term.

Chapter 02: Cognitive Biases and Their Impact

Overview of Cognitive Biases

Cognitive biases in the world of financial markets can be treated as hidden entities, as they influence the decisions of investors. These prejudices, firmly embedded in the human mind, tend to trigger systematic departures from rationality, which have a major impact on the scale of investment expectations. The knowledge of such prejudices is essential to those investors willing to form balanced and sensible financial judgments.

Overconfidence is at the centre of most investment disasters. This bias is observed through excessive trading and overconfident risk-taking among the investors when they overestimate their knowledge or forecasting skills. Overconfidence also tends to set in most often during bull markets when the success of prior investing can swell the ego and tempt the investor to assume risks unnecessarily. Such overconfidence in self-efficacy may become the cause of neglect of crucial warnings, which inevitably cause significant economic losses.

Loss aversion is also quite common, which is an aversion to losses as opposed to acquiring similar profits. This bias has the potential of distorting decisions, as the effect of emotional pain of loss tends to be more significant than the feeling of gain. To investors, this may result in irrational actions like the decision to hold onto stocks that are sinking in the hope that they may turn around, as opposed to accepting a loss and moving resources elsewhere more productively.

The other critical cognitive bias among investors is anchoring. It is the process of using the initial information once met in the process of decision-making. In financial terms, this has commonly been accused of an overemphasis on initial stock prices or benchmark past performance, and this can result in poor investment approaches. As an illustration, an investor may still be hanging on to a stock until it reaches its first buying price without considering other market developments and trends.

Confusion bias also makes the investment environment complicated, as one tends to be attracted to information that will prove their developed ideas or hypotheses correct. With digital media, an abundance of information and a tendency to personalize that information to tastes and preferences, this bias can be reinforced, forming echo chambers. Similarly, investors can tend to selectively gather information that favors their investment plans and sort out critical evidence that seems to oppose that evidence, thus resulting in distorted views and improper investment.

Another pit that investors often fall into is called the sunk cost fallacy. This bias entails the illogical choice to proceed with a task after investing money, time, or effort because of the irrationality to pursue future and present value that was not complete. This can easily lead to the phenomenon of throwing good money after (bad) money, such as investors trying to bail on a losing investment because of the sunk costs.

Recency bias is also important as investors overvalue recent events, usually at the cost of past measures. The bias may result in an unrealistic response to changes in the short-term market and can lead to decisions that do not recognize underlying trends, which are long-term trends.

Realising these biases is the start to curbing their effects. Because individuals understand the psychological processes that are involved, investors can deploy strategies of combating such biases that will enhance more disciplined and rational decision-making processes. In addition to having a positive individual investment strategy, this awareness will lead to more stable and efficient financial markets as a whole.

Anchoring and Confirmation Bias

The role of cognitive biases like anchoring or confirmation bias in the field of financial markets may cause serious distortions in the decision-making process of the investor, resulting in their suboptimal choices. Cognitive bias anchoring occurs when people place too much focus on early information or perhaps certain values, and can take many forms in investing. As an example, an investor may become obsessed with the entry price of one specific stock and then use this figure as a reference point when deciding what or what not to buy. This obsession can lead to situations where a person holds on to a stock until it trades back to the purchase price, even when there is updated information in the market pointing toward a different path. Such actions may result in the loss of opportunities and the taking of inappropriate risks as the investors are stuck with their first impressions instead of working according to the changes in the market.

Another example of the anchoring effect is when investors pay attention to certain numerical goals, like the 52-week best and worst in a stock, without reading into the bigger picture. This may lead to a situation termed as portfolio drag, whereby the retention of dead money positions does not allow capital to be rotated to higher potential opportunities. To offset anchoring effects, the encouragement of investors to periodically re-examine their portfolios with the metaphorical eyes of a newcomer, resetting their price of entry in their minds using the current information reflected in the market prices, and assessing the existing fundamentals and not the anchors with prices distorted over time.

Confirmation bias is, on the other hand, the predilection to seek, interpret, and recall information in a manner consistent with prior beliefs. In this era of digital media, such bias is reinforced through algorithmic newsfeeds and social media bubbles that do the same and remove challenges to the existing ideas. Investors can also be trapped to only read opinions that buttress their stands, e.g., reading reviews on a favourite stock that are bullish, thus disregarding bearish ideas. Such an echo chamber effect has the potential to create bad decision-making because the investors are not exposed to differing opinions and will not take into account the entire range of information available in the market.

Confirmation bias pitfalls can be seen in the recent market trends that caused mass irrational trading, such as the meme stock rallies based on pandemic-era viral misinformation and herd thinking. To counteract the effect of confirmation bias, one suggestion to encourage the investors is to employ actions that aim to find the disconfirming evidence at hand, i.e., to read critical opinions or to have peer reviews under contrarian partners. Bias audits are also advised on a regular basis, as they persuade investors to ensure variety in information gathering, and avoid closure to different opinions.

But all in all, it is important to comprehend and counter-check both the anchoring and confirmation biases so that investors can indeed make informed and rational decisions within the financial markets. By becoming aware of such biases and adopting measures to address these biases, an investor is able to improve their decision-making, decrease the extent to which such cognitive biases affect them, and ultimately improve the outcome of such investments.

Loss Aversion and Overconfidence

The complex and very delicate financial world frequently follows two psychological phenomena that can work to the disadvantage of investors, especially when it comes to loss aversion and overconfidence. Such biases are very deeply ingrained in human psychology and can distort the decision-making process, resulting in less than optimal financial effects.

Loss aversion is the behavioural pattern that behavioral economists studied a great deal, according to which people go to great lengths to avoid the loss of their money rather than they expect in order to attain equal profits. It is not that this aversion to loss is an option of personal choice; rather, it is a strong emotional appeal to human beings that makes investors make some irrational choices. As an example, it is often felt that the loss of the $100 hurts worse than the gain of the same amount, doing the pleasure. This psychological uneasiness motivates investors to retain losing stocks in the expectation that there will be a recovery instead of cutting their losses and reappropriating the resources more efficiently. This tendency is common in the stock markets, and investors will hold onto their falling investments, hoping to see better results, which sometimes never happen.

The implications of loss aversion are serious. The investors can sell successful stocks prematurely in order to make gains available, thus neglecting the opportunity to gain more money in the future. On the other hand, they can end up losing investments because of the emotional awkwardness of incurring a loss. The effect of gaining or shifting towards the bottom examples of performance because of this tendency can result in a biased portfolio that eventually will affect the long-term financial objectives. The apprehension of, and solutions to, loss aversion can be achieved by establishing pre-determined stop-loss orders or engaging in a more learning process with a restrained and methodical investment style.

Conversely, overconfidence is yet another bias that is also omnipresent and might mislead investors. Overconfidence is the phenomenon of over-assessment of knowledge, forecasting, and the ability to judge the situation. Such bias is especially problematic in financial markets, where the myth of control may cause a person to take too much risk. Investors can be too confident after a streak of gains in the market; in bull markets, this can prompt them to take on more risk assets without considering the risk being taken on.

Market euphoria exacerbates these risks of overconfidence as the overconfidence of the individuals is enhanced by that of the group.

The notorious meme stocks phenomenon is one such example: with a general excitement and the hysteria shared through social media, the stock may be overpriced far more than it should have otherwise been. Investors overlook these red flags and invest more in these assets due to recent success, but when the market corrects itself, they incur substantial losses.

The challenge with dealing with overconfidence is to make a conscious decision and ground the decision in reality. This could be realized by adopting various practices, including having a diversified portfolio, frequent review of the investment concepts, and having the right expectations. Also, soliciting conflicting views and peer reviews are helpful counterbalances to overconfidence.

Both overconfidence and loss aversion indicate complex needs of emotions and rationality in financial decision-making. With the realization of these biases, investors are able to implement methods that would counter the consequences of such biases, which will result in more sound and evenhanded investment decisions. Engaging in the path of perfecting these psychological hazards is one of never-ending work, as one needs to be extra careful and always align with the new dynamics of the market. Investors can aspire to achieve more stable and positive financial performance by attempting to understand these biases better.

Strategies to Mitigate Biases

Financial markets are quite complex, which is why people tend to succumb to different cognitive biases that may distort decision-making procedures. In order to comfortably drive through these pitfalls, strategies must be employed to prevent such collisions. The first approach is to inform the habit of exploring and taking into account evidence that disconfirms. The practice is to purposefully seek out views and information that run counter to what one believes or his/her investment thesis. In this way, investors are able to neutralize the confirmation bias, which is the likability of information that drifts towards the pre-conceived notions or the a priori hypotheses.

The use of a devil's advocate approach in investment teams will characterise the other method. In this approach, there will be the appointment of an individual in the team who will disagree and offer conflicting data and opinions about the assumed wisdom. This role becomes essential in overcoming the groupthink process, in which there is a need to have harmony or conform to the decisions, which leads to irrational decision-making outcomes. Investment groups can achieve this through institutionalization of dissent, which will make sure that all potential risks and alternative imaginable circumstances are well clarified.

Small audits on bias are also a crucial component in bias alleviation. Investors are advised to evaluate their sources of information regularly and also ensure that they use diverse data sources. Such a practice will assist in identifying and correcting biases that could distort the view as a result of excessive reliance on a small number of information sources. It is possible to add that journaling can become a rather effective tool to help investors reread their decision-making, recognize the patterns of bias, and elaborate on ways to counter them.

Another competitive approach is the introduction of structured decision-making frameworks. Some of these frameworks contain pre-commitment techniques, which entail that investors make decisions about the actions they will perform in particular market situations before they develop. Such pre-commitments are useful in minimizing the effect of emotional biases such as fear and greed that tend to cause panic choices in the face of market volatility.

It is also important to have objective and unemotional exit criteria. This includes providing an agreed manner in which an investment will be abandoned, regardless of whether it is emotionally attached or in consideration of sunk costs. Following these criteria, investors can determine the sunk cost fallacy, which is the unwillingness to quit an investment because of the time or amount already spent.

It is also possible that mitigating bias can be improved by the use of peer review and accountability systems. It is possible to ask a contrarian partner or an accountability group, which can offer the much-needed feedback and different approaches, disrupting individual biases and assumptions. This teamwork will help to create a culture of life-long resource knowledge and dynamism, which is critical in the case of survival in fast-changing financial markets.

Finally, it would be good to adapt to the use of technological tools that facilitate bias identification and control. Some newer apps and tools include bias warnings, decision-making analytics, and emotion tracking, allowing investors to stay disciplined and objective. The tools may become inputs to remind them to take a step back and think things through before drawing hasty conclusions, and thus teach a more analytical and objective-driven manner of investing.

All in all, incorporating such strategies into their habitual practices should help investors develop more coherent decision-making patterns, deemphasize cognitive bias, and lead to an increase in overall returns on their funding.

Chapter 03: The Role of Emotions in Investment Decisions

Fear and Greed Dynamics

Emotions are usually a key element in the financial markets' sophisticated dance, and they even surpass logic and reason. Two of these emotions, fear and greed, are the strongest contributors to the behavior of investors. Not only are these two emotions potent, but they are also closely connected, such that they are able to provoke each other in a cancerous symbiosis that can cause aggressive movements on the market.

On the one hand, fear is one of the primary emotions that can emerge at the time of uncertainty or when there is a feeling of being in danger. Within financial markets, fear may take the form of the panic of losing money and will end up as panic selling or a failure to invest in a down market. This feeling is not the product of historical financial losses but also the anticipation of losses to come, which equally can lead to paralysis. As such, the psychological consequences of fear go far beyond making irrational decisions that may include selling just when the position is at the most opportune point, closing a potential gain, and missing out on the subsequent recovery.

On the other hand, the emotion that emerges during a period of market euphoria is greed. It is marked by excessive want of wealth-building and frequently results in excessive risk-taking by investors as they seek to achieve larger returns on their investments. Fear of missing out based on greedy feelings of riches can cause market agents to make purchases in overheated markets. It is especially strong in special market conditions, such as a bull market or asset bubble, where visions of fast and high returns may override reasonable pre-calculation of risk.

The relationships between currency and greed are intricate and are prone to high fluctuation in the financial markets. As fear comes into play, the markets will move to sell-offs with investors rushing to close down their positions to save the situation from further losses. This may form a chain reaction where the decreasing price generates more sales, which worsens the trend. Conversely, in environments where the greed factor is dominant, markets may be overvalued as investors keep purchasing at increasing market prices without taking note of the built-in indicators that call forth prudence.

Fear and greed, as defined by Mixa, are key factors that investors need to understand to be able to move through the financial markets to their advantage. Through knowing the indicators of such feelings, it is possible to predict market movement and make quality judgments. An example is where a market rife with fear may provide a purchasing opportunity to the wise investor who can see past the short-term panic. On the other hand, an entrepreneurial market dominated by uncontrolled greed can be an indication that a warning is required, and risk management is needed.

In addition, fear and greed are cyclical and thus sins that tend to strengthen them in terms of occurrence further. This can result in fear, causing sales and prices to decrease. Likewise, greed may cause purchase, further increasing prices and provoking an increase in greed. This cycle tends to bring in the bubble and crash scenarios, so as an investor, it is imperative to take a balanced viewpoint and not get addled by the exciting tides of the market.

The principle of fear and greed should not be limited to knowing how to suppress them in the game of financial psychology, since learning how to control them is also another important aspect. This can be in the development of self-awareness, understanding of bias in the individual, and developing strategies to curb the effects felt by the investment decisions. Through this, investors are free to hope in attaining a particular state of emotional internal balance that enables them to exercise available opportunities and mitigate risks when they emerge, as a result of which, they ultimately fare better in their careers financially in the long term.

Emotional Decision-Making Triggers

Emotional decision-making triggers are critical in investor behavior as viewed in the complex network of financial markets. These triggers, which are mainly anchored on the psychological reactions, can have substantial impacts on finances. Learning about these triggers starts by understanding the basic feelings that drive such decisions as fear, greed, and hope. Although these emotions are natural, they can provoke irrational behavior if they are not treated properly.

One example, such as fear, can make people sell in panic when the market turns. The nature of these reactions is usually motivated by the drive to prevent losses, which is sometimes stronger than the need to generate profits. The physical reaction to fear involves the physical sensation of adrenaline, an increased ability to make decisions, and tunnel vision, the result of which may be the improper evaluation of the situation and its instant decision. This is seen in the case of the financial market in terms of the sale of assets to avoid further losses, which only worsens the situation since many investors tend to sell, building up a downward spiral.

A vice such as greed, on the other hand, can cause investors to employ too risky investments in order to earn greater increments. The temptation of short-term gains can overtake rational analysis, and, as a result, a decision may be made that is not in line with the investor's long-term risk tolerance or plan. This is especially prominent in the case of market bubbles, where the fear of missing out (FOMO) on any possible profit areas may drive people to purchase even at inflated costs. At this point, they will likely incur a loss later when the bubble pops.

Another emotion that is often regarded as positive, hope, may contribute to making suboptimal financial choices. Investors can hold onto losing positions, hoping that the market will change and reward them, or not pay attention to signs (such as position losses) that it will not. This sentimental attachment to investments can be a major drain on your finances, as it may cause one to hold onto these assets longer than should be the case.

Social situation is also a very critical factor in emotional decision-making. Herd behavior and groupthink may increase people's reactions due to the tendency to follow the group and strengthen fear, causing market phenomena like bubbles and crashes. In this uncertainty, investors usually refer to one another on how to behave. This might cause a group bias, and the need for the herd might be greater than individual scrutiny, which could make the decision unsuitable for the investor's interest.

Investors can use a number of strategies to counter the effects of decision-making triggers brought about by emotions. The implementation of pre-commitment strategies (the definition of entry and exit points of trading) is one of the tools that can be effectively used. This is useful in ensuring discipline and avoiding situations where emotional impulses guide one. Moreover, self-emotional analysis and self-assessment may help identify individual emotional triggers, and investors and traders can practice countermeasures to them.

Meaningful stress-reduction techniques can also prove useful. Such practices would help to improve emotional regulation and make investors stay calm and focused when the situation in the market is volatile. Adopting a perspective that puts the focus on long-term goals rather than short-term emotional response will help investors make better decisions, resulting in more successful financial results in the end.

Acquiring insight into how to control the triggers of emotional decision-making is essential in order to figure out the intricacies of the financial markets. Speaking of the influence of emotions and taking measures to control these feelings, investors should become more effective in making rational, well-informed decisions so that their chances of success in the world of finance would also improve.

Managing Anxiety and Stress

Anxieties and stress are very important elements in the world of financial markets, where financial market participants are continually performing under pressured situations. Non-stop flood of information, as well as the high volume of trades and possible financial losses, provide the environment in which stress is like an inseparable companion. Being able to control this stress and have a clear mind and focus is not only helpful but a necessity for long-term success.

The knowledge of the physiological reaction to stress may provide one with information regarding how to cope with stress. Stress will cause the body to react on its survival instinct, or what is known as fight-or-flight, and this reaction prompts the release of adrenaline and cortisol in the body. When it comes to trading, it may result in the desire to make impulsive decisions based on fear or greed, instead of making a rational analysis. Being aware of these physiological signs will be the initial phase of dealing with stress. Learning how to be aware of indicators like the elevated rate of heart rate or shallow breath to remind themselves to put the brakes on emotions and reset the mind can be practiced by investors.

One effective way of coping with stress is to introduce some form of routine and checklists. In another example, a pre-trade checklist can be used as a grounding step where the counterparts base their decisions on analysis and not emotions. Instant trades can be sieved through asking and answering questions such as: am I being driven by fear-of-missing-out (FOMO) or a disciplined approach? Also, post-trade reflection may offer insight into emotional triggers and patterns of decisions, which can create a continuous-improvement process.

Mindfulness exercises have also been found useful in dealing with stress and improving focus. Deep breathing exercises, a few minutes of meditation, or the ability to observe or focus can be added to a trading day. Such practices become useful in establishing a mental reset button so that traders can get back to peace and rationality even when market mayhem is taking place. In the example, such a breathing exercise prior to making large trades can make a big difference in the amount of stress and increase the quality of any decision that is made.

These practices can be reinforced by including technology, e.g., establishing reminders or alerts to remind the person to take breaks or to do exercises that reduce stress levels. When trading platforms are configured to encourage people to stop and think critically, it will help prevent them from rushing into any decisions. Likewise, apps designed to monitor moods or give meditations may serve as important additions to the stress management arsenal of an investor.

This is because the psychology behind investing has been underestimated and forms a central stage in the decision process. Investors can be ready to face stressful situations by developing an effective emotional playbook that contains scenarios of events that may happen in the market. Traders should practice how to react to market volatility, so that after real crises happen, they can become more solid.

Conclusively, coping with stress and anxiety within the financial markets boils down to resilience and even-handedness. It entails the identification of the symptoms of stress, putting mechanisms of stress control into use, and constantly improving the approaches through reflection and mindfulness. These are some of the ways that allow the investors to not only feel good about their mental state but also ensure that they perform better in the markets.

Cultivating Emotional Resilience

Emotional resilience is not only a nice trait in the business world, especially in the financial markets; it is also a major skill. In this chapter, the author explores the complex journey of strengthening one's emotional core to negotiate the turbulent and erratic nature of trading conditions.

To learn how to develop emotional resilience, the initial step is to learn about physiological and psychological reactions to stress. During the evolving process of trading with considerably large amounts of money involved, an increased concentration of adrenaline in the system takes place, resulting in tunnel vision and the process of impulsive choice. Understanding these biological responses is important since it is the basis of formulating responses to reduce their effect.

Mindfulness is one of the effective methods that will compel traders to stay grounded in the moment of trading despite the market fluster. Even such simple activities as a targeted breathing workout can greatly decrease stress levels and make you clearer-minded. For example, a 60-second market breath exercise involves deep, measured breathing before a trader makes a large trade. It can reset the mental stage of a trader, creating a calm state and better decision-making.

Moreover, the need for an organized mental reset button can hardly be overestimated. These include imagining relaxing situations or cue-based mindfulness to quickly get back into their neutral level of emotions when being flooded by the market forces. Traders can use visual representations of the market charts, zooming out to see at a larger scale to put things in perspective, thereby reducing the heat in the moment and helping give the trader a more strategic thinking capability.

The second important feature of emotional resilience is the ability to overcome regret and failure. Regret Recovery Framework is a deliberate model that helps traders work through the emotional consequences of a bad decision. This is a practice of accepting feelings often, learning and taking lessons from past errors, and actively switching the focus to the good effects of prior actions. As an example, the exercise of how to find three positive actions to each error, known as Three-for-One, helps the trader think in a more balanced and positive manner.

Furthermore, post-mortems and practicing self-compassion are crucial to emotional resilience over time. Traders can develop a positive inner conversation by reviewing trades that are not judgmental and being kind to themselves after a loss. This not only helps emotional recovery but also ensures one is better in future performance because one has the capability of taking chances and pursuing long-term interests.

Fear of missing out (FOMO) is a very important aspect of emotional resilience. It is important to understand the social and psychological catalysts of FOMO, such as peer comparison and dopamine rush. Through the use of FOMO disruptors, traders have the opportunity to think before acting on their urge to follow the trend, ensuring that their decisions are not based on hype but guided by discipline.

Lastly, the chapter highlights how fear is shifted to focus with respect to the drawdowns. Through a change in perspective, traders may think of drawdowns as temporary volatility rather than as personal failure, reinscribed and recalculated in the simplified and sanitized investment process. The focus of the practical tools is, on the one hand, directed towards the concentration on things that can be really managed by using cognitive reframing techniques, and, on the other hand, leads to the decrease in panic and increase in strategic focus.

The development of emotional resilience as such is a complex process, which comprises mindfulness, formalized recovery systems, and cognitive reframing methods. Through such practices, traders will be able to build a strong emotional base intensively and not only overcome but also excel in the volatile financial markets.

Chapter 04: Behavioral Finance Principles

Introduction to Behavioral Finance

Behavioral finance, in the context of financial markets, can be discussed as one of the most important frameworks that aims to investigate the psychological determination of investor behavior and the market behavior itself. Behavioral finance does not assume the existence of rational actors in financial markets like traditional finance and instead explores the emotional factors and cognitive biases that cause irrational financial judgment.

Psychology in human beings is an important factor in financial markets. Both individual and institutional investors are likely to exhibit many biases, which may distort their judgments. These biases are overconfidence, which refers to an increase in forecasting where the investors overestimate their knowledge and forecasting skills, and a common effect is that it causes the risk-taking to be more than necessary. Similarly, loss aversion (the pain of loss is more intense than the pleasure of winning) may make investors hang onto losing stocks longer than the probability warrants, in the hopes that they can reclaim lost ground.

Many phenomena, including bubbles and crashes in a market, may be related to group psychological behavior rather than economic signals. As an example, herd behavior when the majority of investors form their views without dedicated analysis can cause prices of assets to exceed intrinsic values, forming a bubble. On the other hand, fear in a down market might further ruin the market due to the run on sales.

Behavioral finance also looks at how heuristics, or/mental shortcuts, investors employ to simplify complex decisions, come into play. Although heuristics are effective, they always induce systematic error. An example of heuristic theory that can affect investment strategies and result in undesirable benefit may come in the form of the availability heuristic on which investors may overestimate the how likely an event already occurred is, an example being a stock market crash that might impact investment strategies in a manner that reflects them being not in line with the actual odds.

Behavioral finance highlights another area that is very relevant to our world today: the interaction of finance and emotions. Fears and greed may become market drivers, causing market volatility at times. Both fear and greed may cause investments to be done very conservatively, selling early in downturns, and greed may cause speculative bubbles when investors are becoming more and more interested in high returns without adequate risk analysis.

Behavioral finance not only attempts to explain such phenomena but also intends to offer measures that can reduce the negative impact of psychological biases. This entails a process of informing investors of frequent thinking traps and encouraging behaviours that would help in decision-making. An example of this could be promoting diversification as a method to mitigate your overconfidence, or creating preset rules regarding your investments to prevent trading emotionally.

This use of psychology in finance has drastic consequences for both the players in the markets and those in the financial sector. By observing and managing the psychological factors involved, it is possible that investors would come up with stronger strategies that consider both rational thinking and emotional factors. Financial advisors and financial institutions can also use behavior-based knowledge in managing their client relationships, a risk management model that translates to more sustainable and resistant financial settings.

To conclude, behavioral finance provides quite a detailed model through which the intricacy of finances may be perceived. It falters on the principle of investor rationality and identifies the importance of psychology in defining market activities. With the ever-changing dynamics of financial markets, the rules of behavioral finance will still work in steering the investors to better-informed and balanced investment plans.

Market Anomalies Explained

Market anomalies are puzzling, thus breaking the conventional applications of financial theory and exposing the complicated relationship between market forces and psychology. These weirding-out tend to take the form of patterns, trends that cannot readily be explained using a classical theory of finance, and this provokes exploring the psychological motors behind the investment decision.

The January effect is one of the best-known anomalies in the market because the prices of stocks go up in January relative to the price in any other time of the year. This deviance questions the efficient market hypothesis, which states that the price of stocks will capture all the present accessible information. Therefore, a stock price should take the form of a random walk. The January effect may also be explained psychologically by the effect of tax-loss selling, in which investors sell losing stocks in December in order to claim capital losses as tax deductions, and then buy the same stocks back in January, increasing the price. This mechanism is also influenced by the inflow of the annual bonuses investment at the beginning of the year.

The small-firm effect is another salient outlier where small firms tend to do better than large firms. These factors may be attributed to the increase in growth potential of small firms, the lack of analyst coverage that will result in underpricing, and the feel-good factor of investing in underdogs. Greater potential rewards can also distort investor decisions by allowing them to perceive smaller firms as riskier, but still have the high potential rewards.

Another anomaly is the so-called momentum effect, according to which shares that have been performing well in the past tend to perform better in the short run and vice versa. This is against the fact that in mean reversion, the prices are expected to meet their averages in the long run. Momentum investing is frequently attributable to the emotional investor psychology, namely the behavior of following a winner and avoiding a loser. This is enhanced by herd behavior, where the investors rush into popular-trending stocks, thereby pushing the prices further up until the correction is reached.

Another inconsistency with the efficient market hypothesis is the so-called value anomaly. Low price-earnings ratio, or high book-market ratio stocks, were more likely to beat stocks with higher price-earnings ratios or those with low book-market ratios. The anomaly indicates that the market is likely to provide opportunities for companies that are facing problems or have a bleak future in the short run. Such companies may be profitable undertakings for value investors. The psychological dimension of this is the contrarian tactics, where a clever investor piggy-backs on the excessive pessimism of the market on bad news by purchasing the cheapened stock up on news, which has been beaten down and could rise in value.

Moreover, there are overreaction and underreaction as peculiarities, which point to the psychological inclinations of market members. Overreaction is when investors overreact to news and make prices go unstable at unsustainable levels. Underreaction is where investors take too much time responding to the news, and the trend continues much longer than it would have rationally expected. These behaviors are based on cognitive biases like anchoring, in which investors become fixated on select details, and the availability bias of recent or memorable events that disproportionately influence decision-making.

Psychology has been the key to determining the market outcomes in terms of finance. With a cognizance of such anomalies, investors might inform themselves on the irrational actions that tend to propel market behavior, and thus afford a chance at taking advantage of such market anomalies. However, to work through these anomalies, it takes close sensitivity to one's own biases and discipline to follow through with actions contrary to popular market opinion.

Investor Behavior Patterns

The complex nature of how investors move in the financial market unravels a fabric of its psychological fibers that controls the making of decisions. Among the front-runners of these trends are the combination of cognitive biases, emotional reactions, and social factors, which define the climate of investment strategies and performance. A complicated combination of logical reasoning and emotional urges will always drive both experienced investors and amateurs. The mercurial market winds of investor sentiment will most often influence them.

The most important aspect of the study is that investor behavior can be understood due to cognitive biases, which obscure judgment. Such traits, such as overconfidence, are common, especially in a bull market, when past successes distort the self-perception of investors and cause them to assume greater risks than they feel is prudent. The social media and forums are described as echo chambers where like-minded people strengthen their views of others in their reinforcing cycle of overconfidence. The popular meme stocks outbreak can prove how the excitement of the masses can set aside caution that each individual has and move towards speculative activities.

Another essential aspect of investors' psychology is loss aversion. The risk of incurring losses tends to dominate the temptation of possible profits, causing irrational judgments to hold on to bad stocks, hoping that they improve or, conversely, dip into profitable ones to bring home profits early. The desire to avoid any loss is embedded deep within the psychology of humans because the experience of losing is more painful than the feeling of gain. It can keep investors in a loop of remorse and procrastination, and they cannot make decisions in dynamic markets.

Cognitive bias, which involves investors dwelling on certain numbers, such as the prices of the purchases or analyst targets due to the anchoring effect, makes decision-making further complex. This obsession may result in stubbornness, as the investors refuse to sell a stock until it "returns to even" and do not focus on the market environment and the prospects in other sectors. The anchoring effect is indicative of how difficult it becomes to introduce new information into your picture, and how important it is that investors should develop some flexibility in their strategies.

Digitalization has intensified the problem of confirmation bias, wherein financiers prioritize information whose interpretation can affirm what they believe and/or ignore conflicting data. This discrimination is even more powerful in the years of newsfeed driven by algorithms and personalised social media content, which may establish localised bubbles of misinformed beliefs. Investors trapped in these online echo chambers can end up basing their decision-making on inadequate or distorted information, and risk increasing the chances of making costly mistakes.

To avoid these psychological traps, some prescriptions are the use of debiasing strategies by investors and mindfulness procedures. Additional perspective can be gained, and the recency bias can be reduced by regular "lookback" exercises in which previous cycles in the market are reviewed. Rituals of being mindful, like taking a few moments of the day in a brief meditation, or writing in a journal, help with Emotional equilibrium and prevent immediate responses to market turbulence.

In the end, the art of investor behavior can only be achieved through a congruence of self-knowledge, discipline, and learning. Investors have the opportunity to improve their decision-making skills and achieve better financial results in the long term by taking into consideration the psychological forces at work and introducing strategies that would address their effect. The road to psychological mastery within the context of investing is just as much about knowing oneself as it is knowing the markets, setting the stage to better informed, reasonable, and ultimately profitable investing activities.

Applying Behavioral Insights

Behavioral insights into the world of financial market strategies can provide a revolutionary way of making decisions and strategic planning in the complex world of financial markets. Investors can harness psychology by learning and applying the tenets of behavior to avoid becoming engulfed in the psychological forces that usually divert markets and individual decision-making.

The psychology of market dynamics: behavioral insights make investors shift their focus beyond the conventional measures and pay attention to the psychological drivers underlying market behavior. This refers to recognizing such biases as overconfidence, loss aversion, and herding, which may distort perception and result in poor judgment. The initial step of mitigation of the effects of these biases is the acknowledgment of their existence. To illustrate, this may make the investors overconfident and use their predictive skills too extensively, taking too many risks. Recognizing this propensity would allow investors to employ their countermeasures, e.g., establishing more conservative risk constraints or technological advice, to overcome this bias.

Another prevalent bias, loss aversion, shows how investors tend to avoid losing more than they make an equal number of gains. This may result in illogical decision-making, e.g., keeping around a losing stock in the hope that it will reverse, instead of taking the loss, and reinvesting funds in more prospects. Through behavioral insights, investors are able to come up with frameworks that can guide them in detecting these patterns and achieve greater discipline in portfolio management.

Also, the theory of herd behavior demonstrates the tendency to follow the examples of the bigger group, often by imitation of their analysis or intuition. This is especially true in the instance of market bubbles or crashes, as collective decision-making is dominated by fear or euphoria. Once equipped with the knowledge of what gives rise to herd behavior, and how to overcome these pitfalls in good order, investors can place themselves in a confident position as to either avoiding the hazards of herd behavior or taking advantage of the only opportunities that exist where the herd is incorrect.

Grounding behavioral insights into practice means instituting formal procedures that institute controls to counter such biases. This may involve the creation of pre-trade checklists to create a binary decision based on analysis, or post-trade reviews to learn the emotional and cognitive influences that may have impacted decision-making. Through recurrent reconsideration of those, investors will construct a stronger decision-making system.

In addition, behavioral insights must be integrated into investment strategies in terms of continuous learning and adjustment. With the changes in the markets, behavioral patterns and prejudices have changed as well. Investors should always be on their toes, update their knowledge of dynamic behavior continuously, and modify their approach to suit the emerging trends and data.

To sum up, the future application of behavioral insights in financial markets cannot be limited to merely acknowledging the existence of such biases; rather, it should take advantage of this knowledge in order to improve investment outcomes. In this way, investors may attain a more effective and subtle path of market involvement, eventually resulting in a high level of strength and success in operating in the financial setting.

Chapter 05: The Psychology of Risk Management

Understanding Risk Perception

Risk perception in the financial markets has an interplay of psychology and real-world implications. This sophisticated understanding of how a person and a group of people feel and respond to risk is at the heart of maneuvering the financial world better. Ultimately, what risk perception is really all about is whether or not risks are based on the statistical odds of market movement, or rather on how investors choose to base them on their gut feeling and their psychological flaws.

Investors usually tend to struggle with the fear of losing even more than their ability to anticipate exactly what will be gained. This effect, called loss aversion, is strongly embedded in psychology and severely affects financial consideration. The suffering related to imagined losses may encourage conservatism among the investors at risk of missing the necessary risks capable of bringing an investor high gain. On the other hand, in market upswings, the fear of missing out can make investors become overcommitted to omitting risks, chasing after the possible riches.

The other important factor with respect to the risk perception is the impact of previous experiences. Investors who have lost a lot of money in prior market declines can become overly risk-averse, which can rear its head in subsequent investments. This anchoring behavior to past happenings may distort the risk evaluation of an investor such that he or she will avoid opportunities that, though risky, have the potential to be very lucrative.

The influence played by cognitive biases can hardly be overestimated in risk perception. Another example is confirmation bias (that may contribute to a case when the information that is consistent with pre-existing beliefs is preferred by the investor, which tends to ignore information that contradicts those same beliefs). It makes the presentation of risk biased because the investors can be misled into bypassing dangers in their investment plans. Moreover, the same overconfidence bias may also contribute to the fact that an investor under-evaluates risks and makes rather risky decisions.

Social perceptions are also creators of risk perceptions. Risk perceptions may be heightened by the herd mentality, by which people tend to respond to the behavior of a larger group of people. When the market is booming, however, there is a group hysteria that may contribute to an overconfidence in risk formation. During a decline, there is a group behavior of fear, which is likely to cause increased risk aversion.

To be able to succeed in the world of the financial markets, investors must understand these psychological dimensions of risk perception. Identifying their biases and emotional reactions allows investors to come up with strategies to control how these elements will affect them in the decision-making processes. Mindfulness and cognitive reframing are techniques that can assist investors in having a balanced perspective of risk so that they can make more informed and rational choices.

Moreover, the incorporation of behavioral insights in investment strategies will provide a competitive advantage. Such investors, being conversant with the psychological basis of risk perception, are in a better position to foresee market responses and place themselves in a better position. The awareness can also help build market volatility resilience as investors develop borderline management of their emotional reactions and focus on keeping their long-term goals in mind.

Finally, the sense of perception of risk is always an ongoing reflection and the process of adjustment. Markets change and emerge with new challenges; investors should also be aware of them by regularly evaluating their perceptions and strategy to keep matching the changes that occur in the financial market. This positive strategy not only allows for improving the results of the investment activities but also develops a deeper psychological strength, which is crucial in the management of success in the financial markets.

Cognitive Approaches to Risk

Within the complex terrain of the financial markets, the human mind is usually faced with a maze of risk and with the mind tools that define mental perceptions and choices of actions and their consequences. The cognitive perspective in risk perception opens a lot of questions concerning how people would perceive and react to gains and losses. Such a belief not only reflects the objective reality but is considerably affected by psychological concepts and biases.

The most fundamental element of cognitive approaches lies in the risk perception concept, which also comprises the subjective understanding of subjects regarding the probability and severity of the risk. To a large extent, this perception is influenced by cognitive bias, which is a systematic deviation of the norm or rationality in judgment. Such partialities are most likely to arise due to the heuristics, or shortcuts in the minds of people, that they follow to make things simpler in the decision-making process.

Among the most effective cognitive insights on risks is the Prospect Theory described by Daniel Kahneman and Amos Tversky. According to this theory, individuals do not treat losses and gains equally, and their choices might be random and not in favor of expected utility theory. The losses are magnified in contrast with gains under Prospect Theory; that is, it is referred to as loss aversion. This implies that the pain of loss yields a greater psychological weight than the pleasure of the same amount of gain. Consequently, people are more likely to experience feelings of loss aversion than gain expectation, and this may cause a person to be risk-conscious even when taking risks could be beneficial.

The other important factor is the framing effect, i.e., the presentation of a situation or information is likely to influence a decision or judgment. As an illustration, a financial decision that was presented in the language of possible losses could prompt a more conservative decision than the externalization of the same decision as possible gains. This shows the strength of cognitive framing as a source of influence on decisions and risk factors.

Another cognitive bias that impacts the perception of risk is the illusion of control. This refers to the bias of individuals in coming up with a more positive conception of dealing with situations and effects, especially those that are mostly controlled by chance. This may cause overconfidence in the trading capabilities in the financial markets, and therefore, it may result in inordinate risk-taking.

It is also a notable cognitive bias in risk perception known as anchoring. It is the tendency to make judgments in an over-reliant way towards the first piece of information obtained (the anchor). This could occur in the investment context, whereby an investor may fail to sell a losing asset in the stock market because he/she is anchored to the price at which the stock was bought, even though there may be new information indicating that the value of the stock may have dropped.

Risk-taking Situations Cognitive approaches to risk emphasize emotion-cognition interaction. The biases that normally arise due to emotions may cause irrational decisions. An example is that when risks are increasing due to the market volatility, fear and anxiety levels may heighten the risk perceptions, causing rash decision-making, which may not be in line with the long-term financial objectives.

This knowledge of the cognitive dimensions would be fundamental to investors who want to make sense of financial markets. Investors can understand the effect of cognitive bias and counter it by formulating superior decision-making procedures that are in harmony with the principles of rational economics. This entails developing the perceptiveness of one-sided cognitive routines and taking measures like New-idealistic re-framing, mindfulness, and rational decision-making systems to improve financial deciphering and performance.

Risk Management Techniques

Risk management, as the cornerstone of the financial markets ecosystem, has played an important role not only in protecting the capital investment of the investors but also in further maximizing the decisions made by the investors in the face of uncertainty. It is impossible to overestimate the psychological aspect of risk management because it is inseparably combined with the cognitive biases and emotional reactions that tend to influence the behavior of investors.

Implementation of effective risk management essentially requires an extensive awareness of risk tolerance. This presupposes self-detection and sincere evaluation of personal financial aims, timeframes, and emotional stability. It is important to understand where one is comfortable with uncertainty since only investments compatible with individual risk profiles can be made. As an example, a low-risk attitude investor may be attracted to investing in bonds and dividend-paying stocks. In contrast, a high-risk investor may wish to venture into the volatile sector, such as technology or emerging markets.

The most important selling point of risk management is diversification. When investing in different asset classes, industries, and locations, an investor will be able to cushion the blow of a decline in any one sector. Diversification is seen to provide a cushion in that it minimises the fluctuation in a portfolio, and thus increases the chances of recording more consistent returns in the long run. Yet, it is more difficult psychologically to follow through with this diversification in periods of market euphoria when the urge to play this gamble with high returns in one asset class is irresistible.

One more important risk management mechanism is to put stop-loss orders. These are price levels that have been set beforehand at which an investor will sell a security to avoid incurring additional losses. Theoretically, equality to stick to these boundaries means that it is necessary to overcome emotional biases, in particular, the fear of incurring a loss or the hope that the losing investment will recover. The stop loss orders are a protection device that helps prevent the decision-making process from being affected by emotions.

Scenario analysis combined with stress testing is an inseparable part of a quality risk management policy. The methods entail assessment of various market conditions that might affect a portfolio so that investors are ready to face the worst. This proactive strategy enables the investors to stay composed during a time of market turbulence since they are prepared and ready to meet that eventuality.

Furthermore, risk management can be developed through the psychological approach of mindfulness, which will bring an element of self-awareness and emotional control. Through mindfulness, investors will be in a better position to identify their own cognitive biases and emotional triggers that can help inform a more well-rounded decision. Such clarity of mind can especially help in times when the market is volatile and impulsiveness should be resisted imperatively.

Lastly, it is always important to have a long-term view as part of risk management. It expects the investors to take into consideration the longer-run popular fluctuations in the market and their overall financial objectives. Such thinking can be exploited against recency bias, where the events close in time matter disproportionately, and can affect the decision-making process, causing bitter investment choices.

Conclusively, risk management in financial markets is not a collection of technical strategies, but an entire process in which the psychological aspects are incorporated. One can manage and comprehend their emotional reactions and cognitive biases, and help investors to control them and navigate the market between protecting their investments and seeking growth.

Balancing Risk and Reward

Regarding the complex choreography of the financial markets, risk and reward are not simple mathematical equations but psychological odysseys undertaken by investors. The promise of elevated rates of returns is always tempting to the risk-taking, appearance, and occasionally reckless approach of the investor. Still, the fear of loss can cripple the calculative powers of decision-making, and this balance has to be struck with ability and perception.

Understanding your risk tolerance is at the center of the trade-off between risk and reward. This is not a fixed ratio; this is an interactive balance between the comfort level of the individual, a sense of what s/he wants to achieve financially, and the ability to tolerate the emotional shocks that come with movements of the market. The investors have to examine themselves well to determine their actual risk appetite. In many cases, the perceived risk appetite might not be the same as the actual risk-taking when under pressure.

Cognitive biases are central to distorting the filtering of risk and reward. Overconfidence may cause investors to underprice risks through ill-misplaced confidence that they can predict. On the other hand, a strong psychological bias known as loss aversion may lead to excessive focus on possible losses to the point of making relatively conservative decisions and potential losses of lucrative opportunities. To overcome these biases, the decision-making process must be guided by discipline, and that involves a combination of rational thinking and control of emotions.

The expected utility theory is a notion that explains the process of decision-making in the case of uncertainty by individuals. According to this theory, the investors give subjective value to the possible consequences and weigh the value by the chances of incidence so as to achieve personal satisfaction rather than the objective financial profit. Nevertheless, this model does not accurately reflect real-world decision-making because it is affected by emotional factors and heuristics, which make decisions far simpler but introduce systematically biased errors.

It is only after developing a healthy risk management mechanism that investors would promote efficient balancing of risk and reward. This would mean that there is a clear investment objective so that an acceptable risk level is identified, and there are tools that can be used to reduce possible losses through the use of diversification and hedging. It is very important to revisit and revise these strategies on a frequent basis because the market situation and personal situation change.

Emotional resilience forms a very important part of successful risk management. The skills to stay unperturbed and focused in the event of market volatility can preempt impulsive decision-making due to fear or greed. Mental skills like mindfulness, cognitive reframing, and stress management have the potential to increase the ability of an investor to become calm and make logical decisions in stressful situations.

Also, the impact of external factors influencing the decision-making process cannot be underestimated, namely, media discourses and peer pressure. These characteristics have the potential to enhance risk perceptions and result in herd behavior, in which the fear of missing out (FOMO) or the responsiveness to peer pressure exceeds the mind of the individual. To stand up against such influences and to stay in line with its risk-reward balance, investors should develop independent minds and learn to be critical in making their decisions.

Later, the scenario of minimizing and maximizing risk and return is an ongoing learning and adaptation process. It demands a devotion to self-knowledge, the ability to stick with a clearly planned investment course, and the agility to change tack as the economic winds blow in a new direction based on new information and experience. With this balance, we can learn to maneuver the waters of the markets without doubt or a sense of aimlessness and fulfill our financial objectives by dealing with the nature of uncertainty in the markets.

Chapter 06: Emotional Intelligence in Trading

Developing Emotional Awareness

The emotional turbulences of the financial markets can be a temporary exception, and it is as important to be able to navigate through these waters as it is to conquer the technical analyses or economic forecasts. Emotional intelligence, which is usually neglected in ways of seeking wealth, has been instrumental in the success of an investor. Awareness of what he or she feels and how it affects decisions can make a good investor a great one.

Feelings are as much a part of human nature as we are to make our choices sometimes gently, sometimes too powerfully. When the stakes are high and the environment is volatile, as is the case in the financial markets, it is possible to lean into those heightened emotions and have them influence every decision. With this realization, the initial move in building emotional awareness is acknowledgment of the existence and impact of emotion in investment decision-making. This means making a deliberate attempt to monitor and detect emotions as they emerge, particularly in such situations of pressure, like market fluctuations or when startling news emerges.

Self-reflection is also an initial stage of the process that prompts the investors to stop and analyze their emotional makeup and not jump into a situation. It includes questioning oneself, like, what do I feel at this present moment? How is the feeling likely to affect my choice? With repeated training, the investor will begin to learn to recognize emotional patterns presented by various market environments. Such an awareness provides a more considered resourcing of decision-making, where the decisions drawn upon are based both on analytic rationale and emotional intuition.

The other important part of emotional perception is knowing the reasons that result in the blow-up of emotions. To provide one example, a short spurt of a wet market may evoke fear or anxiety that precipitates the impulsive selling. With some of these triggers recognized, investors will be able to develop countermeasures against encounters with emotional reactions. Deep breathing, visualizing, or simply taking a break are some of the techniques that can be deployed to help in regaining composure to ensure that when making decisions, one is not operating out of panic and elation.

Besides, emotional awareness entails embracing the mindset that accepts emotions as normal and correct, as opposed to being some barrier that must be pushed down or neglected. This acceptance plays a core role in emotional regulation, where one should not attempt to block out emotions, but regulate them well. Understanding their financial and emotional reactions with mindfulness and cognitive behavioral tips can teach the investors to have emotions without judging; they can then respond to the ups and downs of the market activities in a more balanced way.

There is also emotional perceptiveness in understanding the social and psychological dynamics and adapting to the market. It is important to understand that group emotions and behavior can steer individuals' decisions. Investors should be cautious of the herd mentality when it comes to the fear of missing the market trend, which can trigger an irrational decision-making process. Through the emotional awareness of an investor, he/she is able to counter the tug of group emotions and make decisions that match their long-term plans.

After all, creating emotional awareness is a resilience process. It provides investors with the strategies to manage pressure, overcome losses, and stay alive through market instability. This resilience is what makes experienced investors a step ahead of those who are new to the market since it helps them not only to withstand market pressures but also to prosper under them. With emotional awareness as a piece of the toolkit of an investor, a more thoughtful and controlled level of investing is achieved, leading the way to long-term success within the financial markets.

Emotional Regulation Techniques

Emotional regulation skills are not only advantageous but also survival skills, especially in the financial markets settings where chances that play out the highest stakes are involved. Emotional regulation strategies assist traders and investors in keeping their heads as they make sound decisions despite all odds. The purpose of the techniques is to minimize the impact of stress and anxiety, causing impulses and judgment to be clouded by frustration.

Mindfulness is one of the best strategies to control emotions. This practice stresses an individual being aware of his or her thoughts, feelings, bodily sensations, and immediate environment on a moment-to-moment basis. Mindfulness would also be applicable in the financial market scenario, in aiming to keep traders grounded in the hustle and bustle of stock price swings and breaking news messages. Short meditation periods or some directed breathwork may be included in everyday practices to develop a placid and concentrated state of mind. An example of this is the 60-second or market breath where one can perform a simple step of taking a breath before a major trade, resetting the mind.

Another strong tool in relation to control of emotions is visualization. Visualization may also be applied to help traders envisage a scenario of successful survival in any difficult situation in the market. Such mental training can build confidence and decrease anxiety, which can prepare them for real life. As an example, the trader may visualize how a market chart can be expanded to a longer-term perspective, to avoid the short-term volatility and concentrate on the broader trends.

Emotional regulation also makes use of grounding techniques. The approaches include being grounded in the present moment to avoid being overwhelmed by stress. Applying some simple tactics, such as paying physical attention to a computer mouse in the palm or hearing the general noises of a trading floor, can be grounding anchors. Being centered on these practical aspects, traders will be able to shift their focus from the anxiety-producing thoughts into a more levelheaded balance.

The second critical part of emotional regulation is being able to overcome the losses, including making bad trading choices. The Regret Recovery Framework is used to present a plan on how to cope with the sentimental outcomes of errors. This includes acceptance and dealing with emotions such as self-blame and regret, which are normal when a lot has been lost. Writing a "kindness letter" to oneself is a technique that can aid in the practice of self-compassion and getting past the negative emotions of a trading mistake.

Also, emotional control involves routine introspection and evaluation. Traders are advised to conduct post-mortems on their decision-making process regarding trading and learn from the execution of trades without having to judge them. This reflective practice not only helps to find emotional triggers but also helps to come up with different strategies to manage such a situation next time.

Finally, the objective of the emotional regulation strategies is to develop a state of mind immune to the emotional swings of trading. Incorporating these habits in their everyday lives, traders will be able to achieve emotional stability and more effectively make their decisions to ensure a higher possibility of success throughout their participation in the financial market.

Impact of Emotional Intelligence on Performance

Emotional intelligence and performance are major topics of research in the context of financial markets. This skill area is related not only to the possibility of controlling emotions but also to the possibility of using such emotions so that they could improve performance outcomes and decision-making. Emotional intelligence (EI) in its application to finance refers to the ability to recognize, understand, and manage positive and negative emotions in oneself and other individuals, which is a skill set that is invaluable when it comes to the arena of financial trade and investments.

Emotional intelligence is based on the ability to control emotions. The ability to keep one's cool and composed can greatly impact the way a person performs in the dynamic world of financial markets, where decisions are usually taken lightly and with haste. Emotionally intelligent traders and investors are in a better position to deal with stress and shun the hectic decisions that may cause them to fall into dire economic situations. Keeping their emotions in check allows them to trade and make their investment decisions with a clear, non-biased state of mind, hence the results are more rational and effective.

In addition, emotional intelligence improves emotional understanding and the response to the feelings of others. In the financial markets, it is vital to know market sentiment. Individuals with strong EI are able to read cues in the markets and market moods and feelings, enabling them to get a better grip on market movements and thereby better predict and respond to market changes impacting them. This tendency is exceptionally useful in engaging conditions where market activities are affected by common emotional and behavioral climates (e.g., in market bubbles or market panics).

One of the biggest elements of emotional intelligence, empathy, also plays a very important role in performance in financial markets. Their ability to empathize, therefore, enables them to be more effective in negotiating, connecting with clients, and working in teams since they are able to understand the different attitudes and desires of other market players. This knowledge can lead to more productive communication and nice relationships, without which it is impossible to achieve success in the financial industry.

Moreover, self-awareness, another pillar of emotional intelligence, will enable individuals to understand their emotional pinpoints and prejudices. Knowing how you react emotionally to market changes can save you in the trading and investing environment from making irrational decisions based on fear or greed. Aware traders will have better chances of sticking to their strategies and exercising discipline even during the volatile market conditions.

Emotional intelligence in team dynamics cannot be overestimated in financial organizations. Employees with high EI help build more effective teamwork because people with high emotional intelligence are capable of tackling interpersonal issues and creating a positive, productive workplace atmosphere. This is especially necessary when dealing with individuals in high-pressure environments, as it requires collaboration in order to make timely and effective decisions.

To conclude, the role of emotional intelligence in financial market performance is tremendous. Emotional intelligence helps people cope with their feelings, comprehend others, and be calm under stress, which improves their decision-making skills and results in a positive financial performance. With the further evolution of the financial industry, emotional intelligence development among the employees of this sphere will probably gain even more importance as a competitive advantage on the way to success.

Building Emotional Intelligence Skills

In the financial market, emotional intelligence is not only an accessory skill but a pillar that any investor should base his or her life on. Emotional intelligence, also referred to as EQ, is the capacity to understand, identify, and control our emotions and also the capability to understand and affect the emotions of others. Such a competency is especially important in the pressured atmosphere where trading takes place because important decisions can often be an issue of whether one is made while still calm or under pressure.

The first process in developing emotional intelligence is to set off on a path of self-awareness. This is the process goal to consciously engage in the observation and the comprehension of emotional reactions to the situations in the market. As an example, understanding the fear that may arise during a market decline or the ecstasy associated with bull markets is the initial step in the direction of trying to cope effectively with this anxiety. Self-awareness is considered the core skill of other emotional intelligence skills.

Emotional regulation is what follows when there is self-awareness. This is something whereby the person learns to control and regulate emotions. In trading, that might imply being able to calm down after suffering a major market loss or stay out of a rash decision when experiencing a sudden market rally. Deep breathing, mindfulness, and cognitive reframing would be used as techniques to help regulate emotions. An example will be a situation when the market crashes, and breathing in and out in order to think again and reconsider the situation will help avoid panic selling.

The empathetic part of emotional intelligence is another decisive element in the process of trading, expressed as the awareness of the sentiment in the market, as well as the emotions of other traders. Such a skill can grant traders further insights into the market trends being facilitated by the overall emotional reactions and not necessarily by the technical signals. Sympathizing with the fears and hopes of other investors, one will cope better with predicting trends in the market and making serious decisions.

Besides, traders dealing with collaborative situations or depending on networks in the market should develop their social skills. Communication, conflict resolution, and strong relationship building have been center-stage in the life of trading floors and investment firms, as they have a wide variety of societal needs. Such competencies can be developed by actively listening, giving useful feedback, and always having open channels of communication with colleagues and mentors.

Lastly, emotional intelligence and motivation are also important in determining success in the long run in the financial markets. It is a process that entails goal setting, positive thinking, and resilience in case of failure. A trader driven by both a true love of the markets and a desire to improve the trader will have more capacity to live within the emotional swing anticipated in trading.

To sum up, the process of skill building in emotional intelligence is active and a lifelong effort, one that requires frequent practice and examination. Self-awareness, emotion regulation, empathy, social skills, and intrinsic motivation development not only help traders to become better decision makers but also put them at a competitive advantage in the financial markets. Viewing emotional intelligence through this more holistic lens not only leads to improving one's performance as a person but also to a more adaptable and resilient mindset as a trader.

Chapter 07: Neuroscience and Market Behavior

Brain Mechanisms in Financial Decisions

The complex pathway of neurons in the human brain is decisive in financial decisions. The knowledge about these fundamental processes can provide powerful explanations for why people are likely to behave in a non-rational manner in markets. The risk-reward wiring in the brain is central to this process and plays a major role in the action of the process in financial matters.

At the center of this is the amygdala, which refers to the part of the brain known to facilitate emotional experience, such as hesitation and gratification. Under volatile market conditions, the amygdala has the potential to release elevated emotional reactions and cause impulsive judgment. As another example, an investor may cash in assets too early because he is afraid he might incur a loss, although it is logically unjustified. On the other hand, prospects of rewards may have the effect of overestimating the possible rewards, hence encouraging people to take risky trades.

Decision-making is also complicated by the release of a neurotransmitter known as dopamine, which is involved in pleasure and reward. The flood of dopamine, however, upon a successful trade can give a euphoric feeling, but which, although satisfying, can induce risk-taking behavior. This is because this chemical reaction can result in a cycle in which investors are inclined to pursue the feel-good of prior success at times at the expense of good judgment.

The neurological responses are not independent of each other; on the contrary, they are rooted in common market behaviors. These fears and greed, which are very deeply ingrained in our neural circuits, can result in badly reported financial miscalculation. These are the biases of buying when the prices are high and selling when they are low, or the unwillingness to abandon losses. The market crashes or bubbles are rich in such behaviors, as sentiment is a more powerful way to analyze an emotionally unclouded overview.

One that can be directly related is the 2021 cryptocurrency boom and crash. The allure of quick profits due to dopamine-induced excitement led many investors to the fear of missing out, and led them to invest. However, as the market was corrected, the same mechanisms in the neurons that caused them to purchase at the maximum facilitated panic selling at a loss.

There is, however, hope in the form of the plasticity of the brain. Neuroplasticity is the capacity of the brain to restructure and rewire itself by creating new brain connections. This opens the prospects of enabling individuals to consciously change their reaction towards things connected to finance with dedicated effort. It is possible to counteract the effects of such primitive responses, and investors can do so by developing awareness and using such behavioral strategies as mindfulness and cognitive restructuring techniques.

New, healthier behavioral patterns of decision-making could be promoted with the help of cognitive-behavioral methods in particular. Through daily mindfulness, investors will be able to train themselves to be more emotionally resistant to volatile market situations and be composed and calmer at all times. Moreover, cognitive reframing has been shown to help people treat financial setbacks as a lesson as opposed to failure and lead to greater resilience and eventual success.

To conclude, the analysis of the brain processes in financial decision-making shows that there is a complicated connection between emotions and neural reactions. The realization and usage of these lessons can enable investors to develop a more disciplined outlook on market engagement and eventually have a superior financial performance.

Neuroeconomics of Investing

The complex interaction between neuroscience and financial decision-making is an emerging area that sheds light on the deep understanding of our brain's impact on investment behavior. The essence of such an investigation is that different neural processes control the actions of investors and regulate decisions often unconsciously. The complex neuron and connection structure known as the human brain will process the financial information enough to make rational as well as irrational investment decisions.

Amygdala, a section of the brain that is essential in emotional reaction, is one of the key neurological elements in investment decisions. With fluctuation in the market, the amygdala is aroused and invokes emotional responses of fear and anxiety. It can result in ill-informed decision-making, where investors may sell their assets at a loss due to panic instead of following a well-considered plan. The control of the amygdala highlights the difficulty that investors experience in balancing emotion when under monetary pressure.

The other important neurological factor is that of dopamine as a neurotransmitter revolving around pleasure and reward. The prospect of profit may increase the dopamine level to an extreme, leading people to feel euphoric, which may spur the tendency to take risks. This dopamine burst may prompt investors to sell out on an upward-trending stock or invest in speculative trading without a comprehensive evaluation of the possible risks. The interaction of dopamine with decision-making reveals the relevance of learning how the reward system of the human brain can distort investment processes.

The field of neuroeconomics also explores the phenomenon of neuroplasticity, which is the brain's capacity to rearrange itself by establishing new neural networks during life. This flexibility implies that through deliberate effort and practice, investors are able to train their brains to do different things in response to financial stimuli. Special practices like mindfulness and cognitive behavioral strategies will enable individuals to be more conscious of the factors that trigger emotions and inculcate more disciplined standards of investment behavior.

The primal response of fear and greed, as influencing the brain, may be said to contribute to typical errors such as purchasing at a high price and selling when the price is low in the market. Such errors tend to occur due to the automatic ways of the brain, which react to perceived threats or opportunities. Therefore, the person in charge of the decisions seems to be unable to make sound judgments when making investments. Explaining these neurological underpinnings, investors can at least identify patterns that give rise to such mistakes and prevent them or minimize their consequences.

The example of the actions of crypto investors when the market skyrocketed in 2021 and collapsed soon after can serve as supporting evidence of how herd behavior and irrational exuberance can be caused by emotional and neurological factors presented in the case studies. Such situations act as a reminder about the strength of psychological forces on financial markets and the need for financial market investors to develop self-awareness and emotional control.

To sum it up, neuroscience has greatly contributed to the study of investing and brought new knowledge about the cognitive processes that motivate financial behavior. Recognizing the contribution of brain chemicals and brain processes, investors will be able to traverse the murky waters of financial markets much more easily and, as a result, make more knowledgeable and unbiased decisions as to investments. This knowledge not only serves to improve the performance of individual investors; rather, it serves to improve the market environment at large, stabilizing it and making it much more rational.

Influence of Neurological Responses

Within the financial market context, the neurological responses have been found to be very crucial in dictating investor behavior through the intricate dance that surrounds their conduct. The human brain, as a device of great complexity, arranges the responses that can greatly influence the decision in financial comprehension. Central to this is the amygdala, a tiny, almond-shaped bundle of nuclei that is deep-seated in the temporal lobes. It is a region that plays a central role in the processing of emotions, especially fear and pleasure, which play a vital role in making financial decisions.

Investors whose markets are volatile trigger the amygdala, thus arousing anxiety and fear in many cases. Such a reaction may cause irrational behavior, like panic selling in a crash. Conversely, expectation of rewards can also initiate the release of dopamine, a chemical that is linked to the perception of reward and pleasure. This boost of dopamine may promote risk-seeking behavior, and it can be observed when investors pursue hot stocks in the absence of proper analysis, stimulated by the anticipation of profits.

The amygdala and dopamine are not the only neurological reactions. The prefrontal cortex, which deals with rationality and decision making, thus exercises a counterbalancing effect. Preferably, it can shape affect-related reactions, making the process of financial decisions calculated and less impulsive. Unless under stress or excited, however, the prefrontal cortex will come along to overwhelm the decision, thus making less rational decisions and more emotional ones.

This interplay of these parts of the brain can be the cause of the typical market errors, including purchasing excessively during market highs due to greed or selling during market lows because of fear. Such conduct is usually exacerbated by the herd attitude, whereby people tend to do what the majority is doing because they are convinced that the majority has superior information or understanding.

Delving into the neurological basis of these behaviors gives us a way to minimize impulsive financial behavior. With the knowledge that the amygdala can be used to activate fear responses and that dopamine during risk-taking is attractive, investors can start employing strategies to overcome such impulses. Such practices as mindfulness and cognitive behavioral approaches have proven to reconnect and rewire neural circuits, leading to less and less mindless and impulsive decision-making.

Besides, neuroplasticity, which is a property of the brain that rearranges itself by creating new neural links, implies that investors may be able to condition their brains to react differently to financial triggers. One can develop cognitive control by dedicating time and effort, and through repeated training, the prefrontal cortex will have greater control over his or her emotional responses.

To sum up, the impact of neurological responses on financial behavior is tremendous. The study of the process of how the brain weighs the consequences of risk and reward can help investors gain insights into their decision-making. Such awareness can help limit peak actions and lead to a more disciplined approach to investing, which in the long term can result in more stable and overall successful financial results.

Harnessing Neuroscience for Better Decisions

The complex nature of financial markets has created a need to develop a deeper advantage through neural comprehension of decision-making. The brain, a very sophisticated organ regulating our actions, emotions, and choice of words, is very central to an investor's perception of risk and opportunity. With the investigation of decision-making neuroscience, investors will be able to develop a well-informed approach, as well as eliminate cognitive biases that contribute to the detrimental outcomes in the majority of cases.

The brain is the core of financial decision-making, revolving around the reward system mainly activated by dopamine. This neurotransmitter plays a vital role in processing rewards and, as such, motivating behavior, whereby, in consequence of a high promise of gains, can result in impulsive behavior. Dopamine causes investors to pursue market trends or engage in rash decisions that lack due diligence because their feelings are intoxicated by the hopefulness of reward. Knowledge of the process will give the investors an idea of the impulsiveness that can still occur during moments of market euphoria, which will help them put in place some checks and balances to their decision-making.

Other important factors that affect financial decisions are fear and anxiety, which are processed in the amygdala. In the event of a slump in the market or when it is volatile, the amygdala will also lead to a fight-or-flight response, which could cause panic selling or risk aversion. With these emotional hot buttons in their arsenal, investors will at least be able to devise techniques to keep it together and make decisions more rationally. When the amygdala raises the alarm, it is possible to counteract these impulses by means of mindfulness and cognitive behavioral strategies to subdue the activity of the amygdala and contain this reaction, which will enable one to act more strategically in a moment of upheaval in the market.

In addition, the theory of neuroplasticity provides hope to investors as they look forward to perfecting their judgment processes. Neuroplasticity is the capacity of the brain to rearrange and create new brain connections as influenced by learning and experience. With a little effort of thinking and acting differently, investors may successfully rewire their brains in a way that improves their financial decision-making capacity. This has to do with the fact that regular reflective processes, including post-trade reviews and scenario analysis, can be used to entrench these new neural pathways, which will result in a more disciplined and analytical investment process.

Application of neuroscience in making financial decisions also comes in the form of identifying and overcoming cognitive biases. Such predispositions, the shortcuts in the brain processes, may interfere with the perception and trigger illogical behavior. As an example, the recency bias, in which recent events are given an undue value, may lead investors to make decisions based on the temporary trends in the market instead of the long-term ones. Investors can then understand that these biases are related to the neural mechanisms of the brain and can use counteracting strategies to reduce them, which include spelling out sources of information and systematic decision-making structures.

In the end, the idea of neuroscience application in improving the process of decision-making in the financial markets is only to combine the knowledge obtained about how the brain works itself, and the sound investment practices. Understanding the role of the brain and its effects on behaviors and emotions allows the investor to develop a more enduring and flexible mentality. The decision-making process is thus not only more optimized on an individual level but also leads to more reliable and logical market processes as a whole. The process of constant learning and adapting will help them attain a better degree of cognitive and emotional intelligence, which will ultimately result in longevity in the continuously changing financial arena.

Chapter 08: The Influence of Social Dynamics

Groupthink and Herd Behavior

Groupthink and herd instinct are the admixture of financial markets that creates a powerful influence that minimally directs investment and increases the deal risks. The invisible hand of consensus may seem a desirable thing in the context of investment committees, investment boards, and investment teams, but perilous paths may also lie ahead. This groupthink effect, which produces irrational, dysfunctional decision outcomes as a result of the desire to go along or to be questioned, is especially pernicious in situations where the courage of disagreement is chilled and the comfort of compliance outweighs evaluation.

Consider another situation where a junior analyst with a lot of ideas and concerns concerning a risky allocation decision would obviously feel overwhelmed by the nodding of the heads of many people. The lack of voices that might otherwise guide the decision-making process toward avoiding upcoming pitfalls is often achieved through fear of the lone dissenter, as well as the reputational risk that that position might invite. The fear of opposing views also intensifies the perpetuation of risk. It fosters a type of echo chamber leadership in which only confirming beliefs are considered, as the group, in turn, remains oblivious to other points of view.

The perils of groupthink are graphically depicted in the experience of investment teams that fail to notice the danger signals of an impending sector implosion, caused by a collective action impulse that clouds their judgment about the declining fundamentals of the investment they make. There is also the additional factor of the insidious social forces that manifest themselves in a high-stakes meeting, in which cohesion is prized over critical thought. The risks of losing career opportunities in case they talk against the majority of the members, the consequences of losing their reputation, and the fear of breaking the consensus often lead to a cowardly alliance with wrong choices.

As a countering measure, investment groups must institutionalize dissent as a strength, not something that is detrimental. Among the most suitable strategies that would be helpful is the creation of rotating roles, such as the role of a contrarian in the meeting, wherein the person is allowed and even encouraged to disrupt the perceived commonplace and suggest alternative scenarios. This not merely represents a diversification of the set of viewpoints entertained, but instills a culture of healthy scepticism and/or critical inquisition.

Further, an anonymous internet poll, prior to making irreversible decisions, can give a platform where honesty can be used without the fear of individual consequences. Such an accepted structural methodology provides that every stakeholder at whatever level can contribute to the decision-making process, and this could prevent highly expensive errors.

Exclusive of the walls of professional institutions, the larger financial markets are also vulnerable to the whims of herd behavior. The collective behavior forcefully testifies to the fact that there is a psychology of momentum-following, wherein investors herd into assets that are going up, and tend to ignore the risks associated with it. We can often see this in situations, such as tech stock rallies after earnings beats, in which there is minimal serious analysis amid the buying frenzy.

Investors must be able to identify the tell-tale signs of market phenomena, such as the "dead cat bounce"- a recovery in declining assets- in order to avoid the trappings of herd-like behavior. Such analytical and behavioral checklists may help to determine a true reversal versus transient upticks and give investors the tools they need to make independent decisions.

Independent validation using hard facts and a systematic approach can assist investors in testing the sustainability of market action to ensure these actions are based on fundamentals and not random outcomes of the unreliable behavior of the masses. In a society where constructive disagreement not only goes unpunished but is even promoted, and where critical thinking rather than unquestioning unanimity is the watchword, investors can move through the shark-infested waters of the financial markets with more confidence and with a greater level of resilience.

Social Influence on Investment Choices

In the complex system of the financial markets, decisions on investments are not purely mathematical and reasoned. Social behaviors are dominant components affecting investor psychology, which are mostly influential in shaping behavioral tendencies and sometimes, with subtlety, profoundly shaping investor behavior. This pressure may be exerted in a number of ways, such as peer pressure, use of social media, and the general urge to fit in with groups.

It is a common behavior of investors to be influenced by the thoughts and actions of people around them, consciously or subconsciously. This inclination goes back to our mental constitution, wherein the urge to be socially accepted and belong supersedes self-reliance. This can be observed in a financial context by following crowd behaviour, the herd effect, and market bubbles.

Group dynamics is a key issue of social influence on investment decision-making. It is the relationship in which people copy the behavior of a greater number of people and usually forget their analysis or the fundamentals of the market. Such conduct is informed by the idea that group wisdom is better than personal judgment. But this may cause irrational exuberance, which gives excessive asset prices to levels that they cannot support and is ultimately followed by market corrections or crashes.

The spread and enormous influence of social media platforms have enhanced herd behavior. Social networks like Twitter, Reddit, and Discord represent a contemporary form of the most local of forums where one may share investment ideas and discuss or debate their points, and where viral trends have been born. Real-time sharing of information coupled with the echo chamber effect can develop a hype and speculation feedback loop. The environment can trigger impulsive decision-making, whereby investors may be driven to invest in the latest trend, and worry about missing their gains or being ostracized by not being involved in the current trend.

Social norms and expectations of behavior (what is expected of you) contribute greatly to your investment choices. The fear of running against the crowd can cause the investors to behave in a manner whose path is supported by the current thinking of the market front when it goes against the analysis of the investors. This is especially seen in professional contexts where the risk to one's career and prestige considerations can deter any dissenting voices. Groupthink may trap an investment committee and board, with the resultant refusal to critically evaluate and the resultant risk of group errors.

To ensure that they overcome these social pressures, investors need to develop greater knowledge of their effects. It entails being aware of the symptoms of herd behavior, and it is important to observe the sources of information that influence them. The required ability to think critically and the highly valued doubt are important techniques in determining whether a trend is valid or not, in determining whether decisions should be based on solid analysis and not the power of social language.

Further, the risks of the use of social authorities can be reduced by creating an atmosphere of welcoming divergent opinions and healthy criticism. They can make use of the positive effects of multiple perspectives by institutionalizing the process of disagreeing with the consensus and encouraging open discussions by investment teams, resulting in more effective and resilient decision-making.

Overall, although social influence cannot be avoided as a constant part of the investment environment, knowledge of its dynamics and knowing how to deal with it can allow an investor to make more informed and independent decisions. Using a balance of social inputs and high-quality analysis combined with a clear focus on personal goals, investors can find their way through all the complexity of the dynamic interactions between social inputs to sustainable financial success.

Digital Echo Chambers

The formation of online investor societies has completely transformed the near-virtual environment of the financial markets. Reddit, Discord, and Twitter can now be considered the new power rooms of financial discussion, and information travels at breakneck speed. Such online discussion boards provide both a boon and a bane; they can prove excellent sources of information as well as places of misdirection and group thinking.

The moderators, the voting influence, and the group consensus posts in these online spaces may have significant impacts on the information stream. They can produce a situation in which some stories are given more volume and contradicting voices are silenced. The occurrence has been termed an echo chamber where the repeated mention of ideas strengthens the belief in them, regardless of their validity. Confirmation bias in such closed networks can be very hard to counter because in such groups, only information that confirms members' pre-existing notions is repeated, and the views are further reinforced.

The dangers that digital echo chambers present are serious. They can result in the widespread propagation of excessively bullish reports, leading to the gagging of critics or even the blocklisting of those with differing views, causing a one-sided picture that can be misleading to investors. This may be illustrated by threads in which an excessive optimism is encouraged concerning particular stocks, and in which any critical note or alternative point of view is systematically excluded. This gives a false impression of unanimity, which may mislead the investors to make poorly-informed decisions.

These dangerous waters that are hard to navigate can only be controlled by people who cultivate the skills of auditing information bubbles. This includes the assessment of the richness of their sources of information in a critical manner and pursuing contrary opinions. One of the practical routes of action is to ask the question periodically whether all the information sources agree, and in case they disagree, attempt to search out those that will contradict personal biases. The practice of diversifying the inputs can assist in avoiding being trapped in a digital echo chamber.

Participation in such forums is also important in terms of ethics. This comprises the responsible distribution of information, responsible fact-checking, and not serving any hype or misinformation anymore. The integrity of such digital spaces may be preserved by means of guidelines on flagging misinformation and cues to ask clarifying questions. Through the management of a culture of information hygiene, participants have the opportunity to participate in a more controlled and more informed debate.

Contrarian strategies can provide a route to cashing in on the extremes of the consensus for those prepared to go against the flow. It consists of discovering times of little consensus, where risk/reward becomes most disproportionate. It is vital to conduct rigorous research, proper risk management, and determination to bear the short-term pain as the views change to the consensus. Case studies of the past and present will point out how deals that are not favourable usually bear great returns when the tides change.

To conclude, digital financial market echo chambers are either opportunity- or challenge-based. The knowledge that increases the alertness of the investors in facing this landscape is comprehension of the dynamics of these online communities, with the strategies to counteract their risks. The secret is to have a critical approach, pluralism in the sources of information, and engagement in the online dialogue.

Strategies for Independent Thinking

In such complex financial markets, it is important to establish a mindset that promotes independent thinking in order to deal with the complexities and dynamics of trading and investing. Actively attempting to find and incorporate disconfirming evidence is one of the main techniques used to develop this attitude. This form of thinking contravenes the human tendency to seek information that supports our prior beliefs or decisions, known as confirmation bias. Being exposed to different troublesome opinions and facts increases the investor's understanding of the market scenario and therefore makes wiser decisions.

The second important technique can be associated with the deployment of a so-called devil's advocate approach among investment teams or individual decision-making procedures. The procedure includes an appraisal of the possible negative consequences of one investment decision, pursuant to questions like, What could go wrong? Or: What would occur in the event that the opposite scenario were the case? When planning effectively by taking account of these worst-case scenarios, investors will be in a better position to forethink about negative market trends and help them overcome the dangers of groupthink, upon which a build-up of opinions can be limited as a result of critical thought, and dangers can be addressed too late.

Other measures that investors are advised to engage in include regular bias audit as a way of assessing information sources and the diversity of consumption of market views. This means constantly challenging the possibility of diversity in the sources of information or just duplication to operate an echo chamber, where the information does not challenge beliefs, instead, strengthens them. A portfolio of sources means investors can escape the echo chambers and receive information that they would otherwise never have known.

Moreover, it can be highly effective in developing consistent patterns of reflection and analysis that will help people think independently. This could involve reserving some time to review investment decisions and performance on a regular basis, and concentrating on what was learnt about the successful and unsuccessful trades. These types of reflective experiences not only make an individual more self-conscious but also aid in realizing common patterns in decision-making that may be better or modified.

The application of peer review, that is, a method by which a contrarian partner assesses investment decisions, can be useful as well. This system fosters the norm of positive disagreement and critical analysis and gives a platform where it is possible to put across a challenging vision in a positive environment. On investing, interacting with peers who are pushed to challenge and examine investment strategies contributes to enabling investors to improve their investment strategies and techniques and develop their ability to think independently.

In short, this is a complex matter, and it will certainly call for a concerted effort to promote autonomy in financial markets by challenging existing biases and soliciting a vetting of many opinions. Investors can develop a stronger and less dependent decision-making process by actively seeking disconfirming evidence, having a devil's advocate type mentality, bias auditing, reflective practices, and peer review systems. This is not only helpful in not struggling with market dynamics but is also helpful towards stronger and informed investment strategies.

Chapter 09: Case Studies in Market Psychology

Lessons from Historical Market Events

Market happenings are indelible in the minds of investors. Through numerous market events, there are valuable lessons that cannot be washed away by time and new forms of technology. The above situations act as a warning that market structures may change, but the human behaviors underlying these markets tend to stay the same. The deconstructing of these events can be used to provide knowledge on how people behave and drive the movement of the markets, which is invaluable to direct future uncertainty.

Think about the 17th-century Tulip Mania speculative craze in the Netherlands as one of the first recorded financial bubbles. The prices of the tulip bulbs were driven to extremely high levels during this period on account of irrational exuberance and the ensuing belief that the prices would only increase and would never come down. This development shows the strength of the collective optimism and the way it can decouple the prices of assets from their intrinsic values. The post-Tulip Mania period, in which the steep decline in prices abruptly crashed, is therefore a warning against the risks of speculative booms and the human predilection to herd behavior at the cost of acting rationally.

Jumping to the 20th century, the great depression of the 1930s supplies no less plentiful a supply of lessons. This era of burnouts, prompted by the stock market crash in 1929, demonstrated the destructive elements of leverage and panic selling. Since the stock prices were falling, those who had borrowed heavily to buy stocks had to sell at a loss, and this contributed further to the fall in the market. This incident demonstrates the issue of risk management and its psychological implications on the conduct in the marketplace that fear can cause. It also underscores the necessity of the investors not to be short-term-oriented and to make rash decisions regarding the market signals.

The later entrant into the game, the dot-com bubble of the late 1990s-early 2000s, reinforces the theme of irrational exuberance in financial markets even further. The exponential growth of internet businesses drove the bubble, and technology stocks were driven to ridiculous valuations on projected hypothetical growth as opposed to business qualifying measures. The following crash, which evaporated trillions of dollars in market value, reaffirmed the lesson that, despite the changes associated with technological innovation, market psychology could support market conditions that cannot be sustained. This incident reminds investors of the role of skepticism and prudence, and not being influenced by the hype and momentum of investment opportunities.

In the study of these historical market events, one can find out that psychological factors like fear, greed, and herd behavior are key ingredients in ensuring that markets are trending in a certain direction. With the knowledge of these psychological foundations, investors will be better positioned to be prepared and to overcome the effects of the occurrence of similar events in the future. Diversification, remaining disciplined when making investments, and building an understanding of cognitive bias could help guide an investor through the tricky nature of financial markets. Finally, the experience gained by the previous events in the market emphasizes the necessity of psychological resilience and wise decision-making to attain the goal of successful investing in the long run.

Behavioral Analysis of Market Crashes

The complexities of the market crashes are deeply rooted in the human psyche, which can turn into a mass effect that is often not possible to analyze. In the event of a market crash, several psychological triggers are initiated, and these psychological triggers affect the behavior of investors in a significant manner. Primal emotion fear tends to be imperious as people and institutions tend to suddenly drop their sides in a desperate attempt to reduce perceived losses. This fear represents not only a straightforward response but also an intricate combination of mental prejudices and physiological stress reactions, which increase volatility in the market.

The centrality of all these market dynamics is the so-called fight-or-flight response, which is an evolutionary mechanism that helps us survive short-term threats. This reaction in the financial markets would be equal to panic selling, as the need to get out of what is perceived as danger supersedes the rational way of thinking. Fear on the part of investors and sell-offs at a loss due to fear proves counterproductive, as it leads to further depressing prices. This is exacerbated by herd mentality effects, whereby when people see other individuals selling, it causes what is known as the domino effect, where the more people sell, the more individuals will sell, which leads to the crash.

Also, cognitive biases like loss aversion will become relevant to market crashes. Behavioral finance has documented loss aversion, which is the inclination to take fewer actions to guard against novel losses as opposed to imposing an equivalent benefit. In market crashes, potential losses loom faster in the minds of the investors than future profits, and result in irrational selling. This bias tends to be compounded by the recency effect in that recent falls in the market disproportionately weigh into the forecasting and decision-making of investors who tend to think that a short-term trend will continue in the future.

Besides psychological individual reactions, between the crashes, their degree of intensity is also determined by the social dynamics of the financial markets. The situation when people rely on the choices of others instead of their own knowledge or calculation appears especially prominent in information cascades. This effect can be supported by fast-paced information spread over digital channels, where unconfirmed news or rumors can be readily shared and affect investor confidence and activity.

The part played by the media can not be underestimated in this matter. The panic spread by the sensational headlines and continuous reporting can turn into a frenzy and generate a feedback effect that will further destabilize the market. Facing an overload of information, investors can have difficulties drawing the thin line between noise and potentially useful knowledge, which makes them make quick and hasty decisions, rather than based on wise analysis.

Knowledge of the behavioral foundations of market crashes is important in the development of strategies to reduce their brunt. One of the areas where investors can achieve results is the application of systematic decision-making models focusing on emotional control and thinking long-term. Stress management includes methods like mindfulness and cognitive reframing, which can be used to deal with stress in the case of turbulent times and diminish the effect of biases. Also, it is possible to avoid the herd mentality in advance by cultivating a culture of critical thinking and skepticism toward market rumors.

All in all, although it is inherent in economic cycles to undergo a market crash, being aware of the underlying psychological stimuli and treating the situation as such can provide investors with the instruments necessary to weather the downturns more confidently and with tactful planning. With this recognition of behavioral components of market dynamics, investors will be able to position themselves better to face the next downturn and turn potential losses into the prospects of growth and experience.

Success Stories of Psychological Mastery

The psychological capability can be a well-kept secret to long-term success in a complex world of financial markets. Those investors who have learnt to overcome their psychological environment can turn the misfortunes into stepping stones and create a story of survival and winning. These tales of psychological dominance enlighten how deep the effects of mental discipline and emotional intelligence can change monetary outcomes.

Please think of the case of an investor who experienced a devastating fund close, a point at which one can feel quite tempted to despair and drop out of the market. Rather, this person used the dead end as the power to reinvent himself. Via careful assessment and reflection on the errors of the past, they have regained their career and become even more successful than before, all through the development of a learning mindset. It was not just about financial recovery; it was about reinvention, a new way of seeing the world, and how they should invest in it. It was a show that failed the best instructors.

The next interesting story is of a portfolio manager who waded through the turbulences of a market collapse with a kind of aplomb. As other people panicked, this manager used a finely tuned emotional tool set. They also used mindfulness (mindful breathing) and cognitive reframing to enable them to stay focused and think reasonably in situations under strain. Their capacity to remain grounded in mayhem not only safeguarded their money but also made them score points as leaders who were able to endure the tides.

The examples of such figures tend to emphasize a key element in terms of psychological mastery, which involves the need to turn emotional experience into a strategic resource. Such investors do not consider emotions as a hindrance but rather as a source of information that can be used in their decisions. They also develop a habit of reflective journals and the differences in emotional reactions towards market happenings. The practice gives them a rich tapestry of insights to continue to foresee future emotional pitfalls and quell them.

In addition to this, the community and shared learning prove to be powerful according to these success stories. A large number of psychologically competent investors will be quite active in such peer networks, exchanging experience and strategies. This communal concept not only creates a favorable surrounding but also increases individual development through the commonality of knowledge. The continuous learning experience that they develop through teaching and learning is making them develop a strong foundation of self-improvement and adaptation.

That long road to psychological mastery also involves the tactical application of frameworks and tools that increase self-awareness. As an example, personal dashboards that monitor emotional and cognitive trends can offer the most valuable feedback and help an investor adjust their strategy over time. They act as a concave mirror, and what they reflect is market outcomes, and not only that, but also the psychological processes that underlie this.

Finally, it must be acknowledged that the experiences of people who have attained psychological control in the financial markets disclose a particular truth that can be stated as follows: success is never purely a matter of technical expertise or financial markets intelligence. It is also a product of a disciplined and tough mentality that sees challenges as a way of development. The very fact that investors would look at things that way would help them not only to improve their financial performance but also their personal and professional lives, and act as an instructive example to others.

Learning from Market Outliers

The definition of market outliers could very well be considered a fascinating subject of investigation in the constantly dynamic environment of financial markets, and this sentiment would apply to any investors who want to perfect their strategy and improve their decision-making skills. These outliers, which in most cases are attributed to very large deviations in pricing of assets or market dynamics, can be deemed to be a window through which investors can learn and understand what is really going on in the market.

Market outliers are not simple anomalies and can define market narratives and investor behaviour. They come as a result of a combination of factors such as surprise releases of economic figures, geopolitical concerns, or mood swings by the investors. With these sets of events, investors have something worth learning, on how markets are, and the psychological foundations behind these changing markets.

Another important point when discussing the market outliers is the importance of investor psychology. Visceral things like fear and greed are, in their turn, capable of magnifying swings in the market, and in cases, prices may end up being far from their perceived values. As an example, when the factor that is being marketed is experiencing a market euphoria, then market investors can be over-optimistic and propel the prices to unsustainable levels. In contrast, panic selling of assets as a result of fear may spur exorbitant falls, especially in cases of fear-related panic.

Market outliers can also be analyzed by breaking down the behavioral biases that lead to such a market outpouring. An example of such bias is the so-called herd behavior that entails the tendency of investors to follow the lead of the majority without necessarily referring to their analysis or the fundamental value of the asset. This may result in the development of these bubbles, in which the prices swell quickly before crashing down, as the bubble develops. Predictability of this behavior promotes the ability of investors to foresee a change in the direction of the market by modifying their strategies.

The ability to identify systemic risks, which perhaps cannot be seen in times of stability, is another important point in learning what the market outliers represent. Outliers normally bring out shortcomings in the financial system, like high loan-to-value ratios or poor risk management policies. Investors can learn more effective risk management models by examining these events and taking into consideration that extreme market conditions might take place.

In addition, financial sector outliers may act as a force encouraging innovation and adjustment to the market. They put into doubt accepted wisdom and cause investors and institutions to reinterpret their models and assumptions. Such an adjustment may produce new financial instruments and more advanced analytical and trading methods.

RILEY WHITMAN

A disciplined and open-minded approach is needed to learn the lessons presented by market outliers and incorporate them into one's investment philosophy. In this sense, investors must always be alert and continually re-evaluate assumptions and strategies based on emergent information. This is done by developing a balance between quantitative analysis and qualitative enlightenment, bearing in mind that market action is an outcome of an intricate weave of parameters that may not always be measurable.

Finally, the market outlier's strategy research indicates the need to be prepared to be resilient and adapt to uncertainty. Through the lessons that these events present, investors can further gain insight into the dynamics of successful financial markets and improve their chances of success in a long-term perspective. Not only can this strategy enhance personal decision-making, but it can also be a part of the underlying stability and effectiveness of the financial system as a whole.

Chapter 10: Developing a Personal Psychological Framework

Self-Assessment Techniques

The consideration of the methods of self-assessment presents a complex terrain in which investors are welcome to explore their minds and emotional behaviors in the context of financial decision-making. The common denominator in this discussion is that it is based on the idea that self-awareness is less of a passive act but an active application of attention to the inner most goings on in one mind, aimed at unearthing biases and emotional hot-spots that can be flared up by the slightest slight but which are so easily overlooked and yet carry a lot of weight in generating investment outcomes.

It is through this reflective practice that the investors at hand are invigorated to cruise towards this path and find a way of shedding light on their behavioral priorities. This entails an exaggerated, in-depth self-diagnosis that aims to chart out psychological models, usually by means of rigorous exercises and questionnaires, which explore maze-like facets of their paradigm of decision. These tests are designed to show a person whether he is more of an impulsive person, or he/she is careful, whether they are overconfident, or he/she is reluctant, there is a mirror to say what kind of psychological smit is inside a person.

Journaling as a part of the process of self-assessment enriches the process with additional thoughts, choices, and moods as the source of the journal. Regularly logging the information, an investor may notice the regularities, e.g., the inclination to follow the rules of fear during periods of market uncertainty or the inclination to follow a trend driven by the fear of missing out. This process not only results in clarity but can also be considered cognitive therapy since a person is able to put their thoughts out there and observe them objectively.

A visualization technique is also important in self-assessment, as investors are advised to rehearse situations that could cause pulse-racing scenarios. They can recreate the market crash or sharp rise in their minds and prepare their minds to react cautiously but calmly, as opposed to panicking and reacting to their surroundings. The exercises cultivate an atmosphere in which mental toughness can become stronger, enabling investors to bear the current of the financial markets.

To add, investors are advised to conduct frequent fresh eyes reviews on the portfolios. The practice is a step back in the direct influences of the market ups and downs, and evaluating their investments with fresh and unbiased attitudes. In this way, they can be more aware of such areas of the decisions that may be affected by the presence of cognitive biases (anchoring or confirmation bias).

The peer interactions and feedback are also stressed through self-assessment techniques. It is recommended that investors identify individuals to be accountable to or find communities in which to share best practices and question each other. This outside feedback loop can be a beneficial corrective to individual biases and has the benefit of creating a culture of perpetual improvement and dynamic learning.

After all, the quest for self-evaluation in the world of financial investments is neither a temporary nor an episodic process; one is committed to it throughout the rest of life, and is invested in the psychological development and change, and the capacity to evolve continuously. It is about developing a mindset that should be as accommodating as it is rigorous wherein the person on the other end of the stake should be both the see-er and the seen and to be more effective at his craft as an investor not just in terms of reaching financial success but also to master himself as a psychological unit commanding the motives at their core working in the markets.

Building a Personalized Trading Plan

The development of a custom trading plan is a fundamentally decisive process to take any investor through the twists and turns of the financial markets with certainty and clarity. It all starts with the thorough knowledge of one's own financial objectives, risk resistance, and psychological background. Self-awareness in this context includes deep evaluation of emotional and cognitive biases, which is the basis of a personalized trading plan. Identifying such biases can enable an investor to customize strategies that, in addition to being in line with their financial goals, can overcome the effects of these biases on decision-making.

Another important element of this strategy is having an established and achievable set of goals that are consistent with the investor's risk preferences and time horizon. These objectives are supposed to be specific, measurable, achievable, relevant, and time-bound (SMART), and they act as a guide to the trading activities. Risk management strategy with predetermined points of entries and exits, stop-loss orders, and position sizing principles should also be included in the plan to guard against loss and be disciplined during a volatile market.

When working out one's own trading strategy, it is important to include an in-depth study of the market situation and the peculiarities of the financial instrument. This would entail both fundamental and technical analysis so as to establish possible opportunities and threats in the market environment. Basic analysis assists one in sensing the intrinsic value of any property through economic indicators, financial statements, and business trends, where technical analysis describes price tendencies, chart patterns, and trading volume to reveal the behaviour of prices in the future.

Also, the personal trading plan should not be so rigid that it cannot fit into the dynamic nature of the market. This necessitates periodic reviews and updates to incorporate new market data, changes in personal situation, or financial alterations of desire. The mechanism that investors need to engage is the feedback loop mechanism, whereby investors consistently keep track of the performance and how it compares to the goals that they have set, and they adjust their mechanisms in response. This is a cyclical process that assists in sharpening the plan and enhancing decision-making abilities over time.

What is more, the psychological component of trading cannot remain ignored. The most important aspect is emotional discipline, which assists investors in adhering to their plan even when the markets are volatile. Emotional resilience and focus may be directed toward implementation of the trading plan, in part, through strategies like mindfulness, journaling, and pre-trade checklists. With these techniques, investors will be able to balance stress and prevent making silly decisions that might jeopardize their trading.

Lastly, it might also be invaluable to develop a community of traders/mentors that can be trusted to rely on during trading. Consistent discussion with more experienced traders can open new areas, create a sense of responsibility, and facilitate the exchange of best practices. Not only does this type of co-operation promote better learning, but it also instils some spirit of togetherness and camaraderie, which is vital to long-term success in the financial markets.

Finally, a unique trading strategy is an essential map in the sophisticated investment hall, and it will assist an investor to find their way in the markets in a more organized manner. By considering the psychological profile and personal goals, the investors have a high probability of success that is sustainable and accumulates wealth with time by aligning their strategies with it.

Integrating Psychological Tools

The actively involved application of psychological tools in financial decision-making is a delicate and radical measure that concerns the mental and emotional stereotypes shaping the investor's behavior. When psychological tactics are integrated into the routine of financial practices, the investors can optimize the system of decisions, which ensures a more stable and flexible activity within the market environment.

At the heart of this integration is the acknowledgement of cognitive biases that often lead to investment decisions being skewed. Such biases, as overconfidence, anchoring, and recency bias, tend to mislead investors by skewing their risk-reward perceptions. In order to overcome these biases, one will have to devise a strong mechanism of self-awareness. This includes a planned approach to self-reflection and applying diagnostic (e.g., the Investor Bias Quiz) that assists in identifying individual psychological hot buttons. These dashboard tools allow the investors to understand how vulnerable they are to different biases and thus adjust their strategy accordingly.

Another key point toward implementing psychological tools is to include mindfulness in pursuing investment activities. High-pressure mindfulness skills allow investors to keep an emotional balance as the market is highly volatile. Basic exercises, like a 60-second market breath or a designed micro-meditation, can easily be adapted into daily trading plans, providing clarity and a moment of peace just before making an important decision. These activities can do more than control emotions; they can also help improve general trading performance, as these practices reduce stress- or excitement-driven impulsive responses.

Also, the invention of pre-trade checklists acts as a working technique in preparing emotionally and analytically before making trades. They include checklists that can make investors take stock of their emotional situation, as well as analytical discipline that includes engaging questions such as, "Am I FOMO-ing or am I disciplined?" These prompts are meant to trap impulsive mistakes and make a decision based on a long-term investment strategy, not what is happening in the market.

Another useful tool is scenario playbooks, which offer systematic guidance to respond to any extraordinary events in the market, like flash crashes or sudden price spikes. These playbooks enable investors to respond calmly and methodically to avert any panic-induced decisions since they offer step-by-step action plans in situations of high stress. They include decision trees and the flowchart of the choices and suggested solutions to develop a cool and rational response to the market jolt.

Reflections after the trade even more strengthen the process of assimilation of the psychological tools to transform experience into understanding. Structured post-trade review program helps the investors to examine the corresponding decisions both in terms of emotional and analytical performance, with the scope of creating a culture of constant learning and growth. Chronic reflections on trade attempts (be they successful or not) can allow investors to learn essential lessons and improve their approaches with time.

Finally, implementing psychological tools in financial markets is more than risk reduction; it is a certain state of mind that incorporates the notions of flexibility and resiliency. With such knowledge and control over their mental makeup, investors can find themselves traveling further into the modern world of investment with confidence and competency as they are able to transform psychological knowledge into their competitive advantage.

Continuous Improvement and Adaptation

Competency to evolve and become better is not the quality of the financial market only, but rather a must. Investors must then be presented with new challenges and opportunities continuously, as the world around them is continuously developing with new technologies to be discovered, new laws and rulings to be established, and new tastes to be created. This is a rapidly changing environment that requires investors to be nimble, revising their strategies and mindset in real time in order to remain on the front end.

The reevaluation of biases is among the key elements of the continual enhancement of an investment. Investors are always prejudiced and biased in a way that can impair judgment. With the changing markets, investing should change as well, and the sensitivity of the investor to these biases should change as well. It is important to update your \trouble map\ regularly, so that you can identify and address blind spots that can appear through the emergence of new asset classes or market circumstances. This will be a systematic reexamination of previous actions and results, therefore enabling refinements in strategies as well as in enhancing decision-making.

Psychological flexibility is a major characteristic that distinguishes successful investors from others. This is a skill of re-evaluating and, at times, making changes to one's strategies when new knowledge has appeared. Successful investors are usually those who are able to respond rapidly and efficiently to changes, knowing when they have to change the assumptions they made earlier. This flexibility does not only mean changing direction but also means learn so as to do better next time.

Technology can act as the hinge in this process of perpetual enhancement. As the analytical tools progress and the availability of live data feeds increases, investors have new access to more information than ever before. This mass of data can be a blessing and a curse, and thus it is imperative to formulate effective information sieves. With noise being eliminated and only high-value information remaining, the investor has an opportunity to narrow down to what is really important, thereby increasing the chances of making informed decisions.

In addition, the domain of the adaptive strategies is closely connected with emotional intelligence. Resilience and emotional control play a pivotal role in going through the ebbs and flows of the financial markets. There is a need to devise ways in which the investors can cope with stress and remain calm in the stormy weather. It includes developing what is known as the emotional playbooks that identify how one should react to various situations in the market, which is also effective in keeping emotions under control and not taking rash actions.

Another requisite to sustain improvement is a culture of learning and feedback. This means talking with other students and someone they want to be like. It is possible to receive support and feedback to improve the strategies and stay alerted with the help of participation in accountability circles. Such circles promote honesty and transparency and create an atmosphere of sharing experiences, challenges, and prosperity amongst the investors.

Lastly, it is important to adopt a lifelong-learning mindset. The nature of the financial markets is constantly shifting, and being aware of any emerging development, whether a technological advancement or a change in the world economies, is extremely essential. Improving their knowledge base, investors can always keep themselves and their company in a competitive position and hence be able to take advantage of the various opportunities that come their way.

Effective perpetual change in the financial market really is a matter of proactive as opposed to reactive. It is not only about developing the right attitude to change, but also about being a person who learns his/her lessons, who is easy to change because of them, and who wants to personally and professionally improve. This is not the only method of making an investment level better, but it also leads to investment performance in the long run, turning out a robust and flexible investor.

Chapter 11: Mindfulness and Market Performance

Introduction to Mindfulness in Investing

The intricate world of investing proposes extraordinary elements of navigation across the psychological labyrinths that characterize financial markets in this trading sphere, and mindfulness emerges as a potent arsenal in this process. Mindfulness, a concept closely linked with meditation and self-conscious awareness, finds its applications in the financial sphere: adding a degree of discipline and emotional balance to a financial decision-making process is possible through mindfulness. The secret of mindfulness in investing is the fact that it helps you develop a present mindful state, where investors are able to monitor their thoughts and feelings without taking action as such.

The simplest definition of mindfulness in investing is the ability to settle and develop the level of awareness and clarity. It helps investors to detach themselves from the bustle of the markets and the turbulence that usually comes with financial market choices. The practice aids in the detection of emotional stimuli and thinking impairments that impart judgment and cause impulsive behavior. Combined with mindfulness, this can allow investors to develop a mental 'buffer zone' through which scenarios can be evaluated using a cool and collected mind rather than being triggered to act upon changes in the market.

The art of being mindful in investment involves some practices that are specific to the peculiarities of the financial sphere. One of the fundamental skills is the so-called market breath: a short activity that includes stopping and concentrating on breathing before taking important trade decisions. Such a basic action can stabilize investors, enabling them to enter their trades in a sober and reserved state of mind. On the same note, mindfulness requires the deployment of what may be referred to as mental reset buttons, where the investors imagine themselves taking a break from the direct pressures of the market, thereby acquiring a sense of perspective and lower stress levels.

In addition, emotional resilience is fostered by mindfulness with respect to investing. Due to the frequent ups and downs that investors can experience during market volatility, frequent mindfulness can help those investors cope with the emotional swings. Such resiliency is extremely important to have a long-term mindset, contributing to the ability of investors not to pay attention to temporary failures and aim at their general financial agenda. The capacity to stay calm and focused during the market crashes speaks volumes about the power that mindfulness can bring to the psychological tool set of an investor.

It seems that mindfulness may help to promote the significant improvement of investment performance due to the generation of emotional stability and limitation of the impact of cognitive biases. Research has demonstrated that mindful investors are better protected against stress and better informed decisions, and are less likely to experience the pitfall of emotional decision-making. Not only will such a technique enhance the performance of the individual investments, but it will also help create a steadier and reasonable environment in the market in general.

Mindfulness is not the easiest addition to investing. It demands discipline in practicing on a regular basis and being willing to grapple with our inner prejudices and emotional reflexes. Nevertheless, the positive effects of such practice are largely in-depth, and it provides a trajectory suggesting a higher likelihood of self-discovery and sharper decisions. Incorporating the concept of mindfulness, an investor may alter his or her behavior on the financial market stage, switching to a more mindful approach to problems and finding ways to apply it in the manner of a self-disciplined human being who focuses on the wisdom of thinking rather than being brash.

In the final analysis, though, mindful investing is a much more considerate approach to the investing aspect of the markets, where judgments are not rushed but well-informed of the market itself as well as the psychological state of the researcher. Such a holistic strategy does not just improve individual well-being but also is the key to ensuring lifelong financial prosperity.

Practical Mindfulness Techniques

Within the dynamic and at times overwhelming environment of financial markets, the integration of mindfulness-based techniques can be a life-altering practice to support professionals in ensuring clarity and composure. Modernizing traditional mindfulness and matching it with the high-tempo environment of the financial world implies establishing practical, concise practices, which can be incorporated into everyday life easily.

Mindfulness refers to a level of understanding in the present, which can be a very demanding yet rewarding part of trading or financial decision-making. The 60-second market breath exercise involves a fast activity that helps traders figure out how to anchor themselves prior to making an important trade. This includes a pause to concentrate on the breath and allows time to disengage from the frantic rush of information and feeling.

Micro-meditations are helpful to people in highly stressful positions. Such short guided sessions could be done then in one place, at the desk, which can be both in the office and outside of it. Focused breathing, body scans, or mindful observation are techniques that anchor people within and make them less stressed and more decision-making. Being mindful of the ambient noise of a trading floor (an example) can be used as a grounding practice to refocus attention to the present, rather than being worried about what tomorrow will bring.

Another component of mindfulness is looking out for or paying attention to the small signals that could be missed in the rush of trading. By way of example, awareness of physical tension in the hand just prior to clicking sell may cause one to reflect and thus prevent making rash decisions. Awareness of this sort can translate into more conscious decisions.

One element of mindfulness in finance is what is known as the mental reset button procedure, and it is performed during overarching times or when one feels overwhelmed and seeks a form of reprieve. This includes cue-based or visualizing mindfulness, which is a quick way of going back to neutrality. In order to think more strategically, traders can look at a market chart zoomed out to a one-year look, so that they have some perspective and are not influenced by short-term volatility.

Mindfulness can decrease stress immediately, but this is not all; mindful practices also lead to the reduction of stress and increase performance and emotional stability. Mindfulness practices also improve trading results, as it has been demonstrated in studies that it leads to better emotional balance, which plays a significant role in keeping trading stocks resilient in turbulent markets.

By integrating these techniques of mindfulness into everyday life, one not only benefits from stress control but also improves overall performance in the market. By being present and mindful, financial professionals cannot only navigate the complexities of their environment more easily and more effectively but also, through it all, eventually end up with more successful results.

Impact of Mindfulness on Decision-Making

Within the pressure-packed financial markets where multi-million dollar decisions are made in split seconds, high-stakes place important considerations on mindfulness as a means of improving the decision-making process. The practice of mindfulness, which has been discussed since ancient times as a kind of meditation, may serve to bring some clarity and calm as an essential feature of the ability to make decisions in turbulent conditions.

Mindfulness teaches an individual to stay in the present and promotes an increased level of awareness and attention. That is the state of awareness that enables investors and other financial professionals not to react to their thoughts and feelings, but gives a space between the stimulus and the response, which is the way in which they are able to observe them. Such a space will allow a more considered and cerebral process of decision-making to occur, and be less prone to rash behaviour born of fear or greed.

The mindfulness technique assists in spotting and recognizing the different prevailing cognitive prejudices that tend to blur judgment. Financial professionals will be able to identify overconfidence, loss aversion, and herd mentality by adopting an open curiosity/acceptance attitude. It is a beginner treatment to their influence as the decisions no longer get driven by subjective emotion, but rather by careful analysis and thought.

Further, mindfulness helps in relieving stress, which is important in high-pressure areas such as trading floors. The capability of remaining calm and thinking when there is market turbulence can promote more logical decision-making because the factors that induce stress are likely to initiate the fight-or-flight response, thus influencing irrational behavior that might not be in tandem with long-term strategic plans. The practice of mindfulness through focused breathing and body scans would assist in slowing down the nervous system, therefore, achieving a state of relaxed alertness, which is ideal in making effective decisions.

Mindfulness may also be introduced into a new routine to develop control and attention, which are important features when working with financial reports and the analysis of market trends. With a consistent mindfulness practice comes increased attention spans and the ability to continue to focus on the tasks without becoming distracted by market noise and information irrelevance. Such increased attention enables market conditions and trends to be analysed to a greater degree, and thus better-informed investment decisions can be made.

Also, mindfulness promotes emotional intelligence, which is a key ingredient to successful leadership and decision-making. Making financial leaders more aware of their feelings and the emotions of those around them will help them achieve better communications, develop stronger relationships, and overall make the workplace less competitive. Such an awareness of emotional conditions also proves useful in predicting how the market is going to react and the psychological impulses causing shifts in the market.

The effects of mindfulness are far-reaching and go beyond affecting the individual decision also to affect the organizational culture. Organizations that encourage the activity of mindfulness tend to indicate the increasing rates of employee satisfaction, lower stress, and the rise of productivity. An organization that has a culture of mindfulness can improve the way it makes decisions across the board and achieve high performance and a competitive edge.

Altogether, mindfulness provides a powerful concept that can be utilized to advance judgment in the financial markets. Similar to the creation of a mindful state of calm, aware presence, mindfulness can assist individuals and organizations in making sense of the financial world by advancing the clarity and effectiveness of their actions. With the market needs constantly changing, the role of the incorporated mindfulness practices is likely to become an inseparable part of financial strategic decision-making processes.

Building a Mindful Trading Routine

In the high-pressure environment of financial markets, a robust and carefree mind is thus paramount to coming up with sound decisions when making trades. The key is finding a mindful trading routine, a routine that brings awareness and intentional practice into the trading day. Such a method not only makes the decision-making process more acute but also teaches how to remain emotionally stable in the conditions of constant changes and turns in the markets.

Starting a mindful trading routine starts with an intentional beginning of each trading session in mind. This will be done by taking a few moments before the market is opened to do some introspection of one's goals and to develop a sense of being. With this tighter intent, traders will find it easier to align their actions to be in line with their long-term goals rather than being distracted by short-term noise in the market. This mindfulness applied may also require only half a minute to take a little bit of meditation or deep breathing, a way to reset the mind to the right baseline, where it can begin to operate.

Another important factor is to include disciplined breaks during the course of the trading day. These pauses act as a chance to get off the screens to enable traders to rest and refocus their minds. These moments can be a stress reliever, as well as support and avoid burnout, whether it is a short walk, a moment of mindfulness, or a change of scenery. They are also an opportunity to consider the events of the morning, check the level of emotions, and adjust the plans, correcting them in case of errors.

A journal is a gold mine in the mindful trading regimen, a realm to record reflection, feelings, and observations. As traders record on a regular basis, they will be able to understand their emotional triggers and behaviour patterns better. The practice not only assists in checking the list of repeated errors, but it also indicates the strategies that were undertaken, which have been successful, leading to continuous improvement. A developed trading journal is a personal guide with lessons from historical experiences and becomes a point of reference when making decisions in the future.

Mindfulness is also visible in the manner in which traders relate to information. This is especially crucial in the age of a market overloaded with information, and behavior that should have an intentional process of consuming information in this market. This implies creating parameters about what and how much information is being consumed, with high priority on high-value, pertinent data that will aid in decision-making and not interfere with it. Adopting a more disciplined news and data consumption posture will aid in keeping the focus and lessening the pecuniary toll of trading emotion.

Last but not least, peer influence and responsibility are relevant in upholding a mindful trading habit. Connecting with other traders sharing similar interests can give an individual encouragement and motivation, with a suitable context of exchanging experiences and approaches. Check-ins with accountability partners can reinforce and maintain the positive habits and serve as a sounding board for ideas, so traders stay on track and remain mindful of their goals.

Incorporating these aspects in everyday life will help traders develop a stable structure that will facilitate not only their psychological fitness but also their economic goals. Not only will a mindful trading routine increase performance, but it will also lead to a more balanced and satisfying approach to financial trading.

Chapter 12: Harnessing Technology for Psychological Insight

Digital Tools for Behavioral Analysis

Within the environment of the financial markets, where decisions are frequently taken (in less than a second), the utilization of digital tools to analyze the behaviour has become a key element that investors within the industry explore in order to enhance their decision-making process. The reason is that these tools are developed to help reveal and better understand the psychological impulses, which are usually obscured, motivating the market. Insight based on such discoveries can result in more rigorous and successful investment decisions.

Behavioral analysis Digital tools include a far-ranging ecosystem of applications, with some as simple as real-time emotion and bias tracking apps to sophisticated platforms that provide dashboard access to behavioral alerts. Such tools are used to detect and gauge the psychological variables that might affect the investment choices of an investor; these relevant variables include fear, greed, and excessive optimism. Through the use of technology, investors are able to better understand their behavioral patterns themselves, which will help them recognize tendencies that could cause them to make bad decisions in response to stress.

Tracing of biases and emotional states is one of the key forms of application of these digital tools. The use of bias tracker applications enables investors to record their emotional reactions to events in the market, enabling a history to be recorded, which can then be analyzed, and potential patterns and triggers may be determined. This self-knowledge is essential in an industry where emotional responses may tend to obscure judgment, thereby resulting in improper investment decisions. Through observation of these logs, the investors are able to forge measures to correct the harm the negative emotions could cause to their trading operations.

In addition, the digital dashboards also provide a holistic overview of an investor's portfolio, coupled with behavioral alerts that would inform users that they may have certain biases that influence their trades. These dashboards are customizable to receive automated reminders and alerts on pre-trade checklists, post-trade reviews, and recording of the emotional states. These characteristics will promote the aspect of waiting and thinking before making choices, and investors will learn to be disciplined and thoughtful in their actions.

Another important merit of digital tools in behavioral analysis is the incorporation of the tools in contemporary financial platforms. Integration with brokerage accounts, calendars, and note-taking programs can be synced, so that the insights of behavioral analysis can become a part of the daily routine of a trader. Indicatively, reflection templates may be associated with the calendar reminder, which stimulates the regular analysis of performance in emotional and analytic terms.

Security and privacy of using digital tools in the analysis of behavior are also key issues. Investors will need to be at ease because their information is safe and their psychological information is confidential. Security is built into the tools to guarantee that the confidential information concerning biases and emotional conditions is secure.

After all, behavioral analysis tools can help investors construct a stronger psychological foundation to be capable of making better-informed decisions that are rational even under the most turbulent market conditions. Investors can therefore develop a competitive advantage by manipulating their individual psychological reactions to situations (by becoming self-aware), turning their weaknesses to their disadvantage, and turning their strengths that can contribute to overall success in the world of financial markets in the long run.

Using Apps to Track Emotions

Feelings tend to take center stage in decision-making in financial markets that are characterized by stiff competition. With the introduction of technology, many tools have been introduced to allow investors to control their emotions, and applications that can specifically be used to track emotions have gained high usage. These are digital tools that allow the user to track and review how he or she feels in the marketplace, and this information may prove important in making a better decision in terms of investment.

Their main workplace is emotional awareness, as the applications help the user identify patterns in their emotional reaction to various financial situations. Putting the feeling down at various times or to a particular market event, the investor can start to get a picture of how an emotion like fear, greed, or overconfidence can affect their decisions to trade. Such awareness is the initial process of combating the ill effects of emotional bias.

A significant number of these applications facilitate mood-setting features, which allow the user to document his/her moods daily or as a response to changes in the market. Other apps take the form of graphs illustrating changes in emotional levels over a period of time and let the user picture the nature of their path and see what makes them act impulsively. By noting these tendencies, investors will be able to find strategies that will help them more closely control their reactions with the goal of becoming more consistent and rational in the way they approach trading.

The next valuable attribute of emotion-tracking apps is the delivery of time-sensitive alerts and reminders. These may be adapted to remind users at important times, e.g., just before making a trade, to stop and evaluate how they feel. This delay may help avoid rash actions based on a momentary emotional situation and make people rethink what they are doing within the boundaries of their long-term financial plans and strategies.

Therefore, there are fully developed apps, which are combined with other tools and platforms, such as trading dashboards or personal calendars, to provide an essential experience. With this integration, a more thorough and complete option for managing emotion can be established because the user can now correlate their emotional information with their trading process and have a comprehensive picture of how emotions can affect their trading. The association of emotional insights with the actual trading performance allows users to improve their perception of the impact of their emotional states on their financial performance.

Emotion-tracking apps should focus especially on data privacy and security. Numerous applications focus on privacy functionality to ensure the privacy of emotional data that individuals may have stored. Such a guarantee is important to make users feel free to enter sensitive data about their emotional conditions, without which this app cannot work effectively.

The idea is such that the emotion-tracking apps act as a personal coach and direct users so that they can be more emotionally intelligent in their investment decisions. Through increased self-awareness and emotional control, such tools can assist investors in avoiding the most common trappings of emotional trading, including panicked selling or staying in a losing position due to fear. With the continuous changes in the financial markets, it is predicted that the importance of technology in guiding investors to pay emotional discipline is expected to increase, and these apps are becoming an unavoidable feature of the toolbox of a modern investor.

Integrating AI in Trading Psychology

The incorporation of artificial intelligence into trading psychology is one of the key changes happening in the potentially rapidly changing stage of the financial market. This is not just a technological revolution, but it also significantly changes the emotional and cognitive dynamics that traders are exposed to. AI technology and its ability to process large amounts of data and determine the patterns that humans cannot, provide an additional level of trading psychology and greatly improve trading decision-making algorithms, although, at the same time, it brings various challenges.

Artificial intelligence can be used as a potent aid in countering cognitive biases that have bedeviled traders over time. Using the historical data and current information, AI systems may recognize patterns of emotional decision-making, including overconfidence or loss aversion, and give traders that will support with evidence-based feedback. This feedback structure can make traders aware of their biases, reflecting their emotional conditions, and lead towards more rational decision-making. Likewise, AI may notify the traders that their judgments are being subject to recency bias, which causes a disproportional influence of the events that occurred in the past, tainting their judgment and, therefore, reminding them to consider such long-term tendencies more.

Additionally, the simulation capacity of AI gives traders an exclusive chance to prepare their reactions to different market situations. These simulations may consist of stress-testing portfolios against imaginary market crashes or rallies, and enable the trader to experience how his/her emotions and strategies react, and to improve these strategies without risking real money. It not only tempers the traders to the volatility of the real world market but also conditions them to emotions by lessening the shock and stressful feelings that the unexpected happenings in the market can engender.

Nevertheless, there are also difficulties in adopting AI in the psychology of trading. Among the concerns is the possibility of a decline in the use of AI systems. Traders can end up relying too heavily on algorithmic suggestions, where they turn to using their instinct or being able to read the market that AI potentially missed. This dependency may cause the loss of the emotional pulse of the market, which tends to play a crucial role in the comprehension of the market attitude and forecasting changes.

Moreover, one must not disregard the moral perspective of AI in the psychology of trading. The implementation of AI systems prompts the concern about whether they are safe in terms of data privacy and the possibility of manipulation. To cope with these ethical implications, traders and firms should strive to employ AI to complement the decisions made by human beings, not as a means of replacing human decision-making capabilities and taking advantage of gaps in the marketplace.

Finally, a technology such as AI in trading psychology is a two-edged sword. Although it can provide immense value in the levels of bias reduction, decision making, and emotional resilience, it has to be balanced correctly to ensure that human intuition and ethics are not lost. When traders move on to this new realm of experience, attention must be on the establishment of a synergistic interaction with human power of intuition and technological powers of automation, taking advantage of the technology to augment the understanding of the human mind without betraying the foundations of ethical trade and human capacity to judge. This trade-off will outline the future of trading psychology, with AI acting as a leader and a watchdog of rational and ethical investment behaviours.

Future of Technology in Behavioral Finance

Technology is becoming a major driver in behavioral finance in the fast-changing environment of financial markets. This point of convergence between technology and finance not only transforms the way that markets are conducted but also the way individual investors make decisions. As we head towards this future, a number of important trends are appearing, each of which has immense consequences for the psychology of investing.

The latest trends and the forefront of this shift include artificial intelligence (AI) and machine learning. Such technologies are facilitating the processing of enormous sets of information in an unprecedented frame of time, offering visibility that could not be gained before. It is now possible to use algorithms to identify patterns and anomalies in the trading behavior, potentially implying errors in emotional biases or irrational decision-making. The potential of this ability to inform market trends and orient investor behaviors to act more advantageously is enabling financial players to predict better market trends and shifts, strategize, and formulate tactics accordingly.

Besides, AI-powered platforms are growing more customized in order to provide custom investment recommendations based on a customer-specific psychological profile. This customization is enabled by highly advanced data analysis, taking into consideration the historical actions of the investor, risk appetite, and even mood. These tools are capable of making the user rethink short-term decisions, thereby instilling greater discipline in the process of investment.

Another technological innovation that influences behavioral finance is the growth of blockchain and cryptocurrencies. These non-centralized platforms not only change the mechanics of transactions but also work on the psychology of investors. Blockchain transparency and security can contribute to an increase in financial system trust. Still, blockchain systems associated with cryptocurrencies have cost-related volatility that can strengthen existing behavioral biases like fear of missing out (FOMO) and herding. Consequently, the efforts to devise mechanisms that counter such biases by investors, in relation to digital currencies, are on the increase.

The growth of trading mobile apps and social media also had an extensive effect on influencing investor behavior, creating trends and patterns of behavior. These media give access to market information and peer judgment in real time, which is both a curse and a blessing. Although they bring democratization of access to financial markets, they still increase the impact of social proof and confirmation bias. Investors are more likely to follow the trend and make this decision based on the actions of other people and not their own research. This fact stresses the significance of incorporating the understanding of behavior into the development of such platforms to facilitate healthier investment behavior.

Also, the addition of virtual reality (VR) and augmented reality (AR) into financial education and trading simulation provides an opportunity to teach investors in new ways. These technologies can also assist these individuals in knowing how to handle their emotional reactions to the rise and fall in the market since they put them into more realistic market contexts and are therefore better equipped to make decisions under the circumstances.

With the future of technological innovations in behavioral finance being unraveled, it is of great importance that individuals who invest in the financial market, as well as the professionals themselves, need to adjust to the changes. Adopting the use of technological advances would make the decision-making process more efficient; however, it will also demand a greater level of understanding of the psyche behind all that is happening. Nowadays, through the intelligent use of technology, it is possible not only to maximize the financial performance of the investors but also to possess a higher level of emotional stability when facing the fluctuations of the market. This is the developing environment, and challenges and opportunities include the need to develop a proactive approach to combining technology with behavioral finance initiatives.

Chapter 13: Building a Crisis-Ready Mindset

Preparing for Market Volatility

Volatility is one such virtual presence that has dogged the financial markets in the ever-changing environment, and it must be managed well using skill and foresight by the investors. There are further instances where the market may be highly unpredictable. Therefore, the trader may experience a raft of emotions, from anxiety to excitement, as even the most market-experienced investors have been known to lose their composure. Learning to deal with these changes and planning on how to counter them is vital in risk elimination and the exploitation of the opportunities.

Many sources cause market volatility. Large price moves may be caused by economic data, geopolitical factors, or even changes in investor sentiment. As an example, consider how a sudden rise or drop in interest rates or unstable politics has a shock effect throughout the markets, causing either a buying or selling spree. On the same note, developments and innovations on the technological front have the potential to interfere with an already existing industry, prompting a sudden change in valuation.

Investors should build their knowledge about the inner workings of the market, which will guide price fluctuations, so that they can prepare to withstand such bouts of volatility. This doesn't only mean being updated with what is going on out there, but also means examining historical data to spot trends and patterns. By identifying the likely volatility signs, investors are in a position to either defend their portfolios or jump into the newly discovered opportunity.

Diversification is one of the major tricks to deal with market volatility. Through investment diversification according to asset classes, sectors, and geographies, investors are able to minimize the effect of any individual event in the market on the overall portfolio. This will give an opportunity to balance the risk and reward aspect, whereby gains in one segment can recompense the loss in another.

Additionally, it is important to keep the investment strategy strict. Market volatility can cause you to make emotional decisions that result in expensive mistakes. Equally, panic selling in a downturn or buying because of an exuberant rally can eat into the long-term returns. Thus, it is better to conceive investment objectives and adhere to a well-considered plan so that investors will not feel like acting impulsively.

Investors are also advised to have stop losses that will help manage the risk they face as they invest. These mechanisms may automatically trigger the sale of a security when it hits a specified price, and hence minimize any losses incurred. They may also find periodic portfolio reviews and portfolio adjustments to help keep investments on track with market conditions, as well as life-changing events.

Besides all these technical strategies, psychological resilience is quite a large part of withstanding market volatility. One of the skills that investors should acquire is to remain calm and pay attention even in times when the market is turbulent. This can be attained by practicing mindfulness, stress management, and a long-term investment life outlook.

The key points and takeaways, ultimately, however, prepping against market volatility is all about establishing a firm skeleton that comprises good investment principles and psychological strength. In this way, investors can not only preserve their wealth but also be prepared to take advantage of the situation generated by the changes in the market. With the financial world still changing, individuals who are better equipped will stand a better chance of confronting the onset of uncertainty.

Crisis Management Techniques

In the core of fixed markets, where unpredictability prevails, the skill of managing crisis is one of the markers of an investor-heroism and tactical performance. Crisis management in the financial market is a very multifaceted landscape as it requires a mixture of psychological thinking, strategic decision-making, and computer integration.

The key to good crisis management is to have a swift action protocol in place when faced by a situation involving acute stress. This includes a short routine to calm down and help achieve a level head in making decisions in market mayhem. A five-step guide may help to stay clear and focused: stop, breathe, name the emotion, check the facts, and determine a delay. This kind of protocol helps not only to ground the investor in the present but also helps with adrenaline-fueled reactions as well.

Complemented by psychological anchoring, physical activities act as short-term stress release tools, and assist in maintaining presence of mind and calm. Short activities, such as touching five items on the table, counting backwards 100-7, etc., can pull the mind out of the panic to restore clear thought. They are grounding techniques in the sense that they serve as a transition between a turbulent state of volatility-induced chaos and a calm state of reflection on the part of the investor.

Technology plays the role of improving the effectiveness of such routines. To enable traders to have easy access to these techniques when they are most needed, one can use phone alarms or digital reminders that are set up to remind traders about these techniques between the times of scheduling trades or after there has been an important piece of news. This technology fortification not only contributes to the timeliness of the use of crisis management strategies but also creates a culture of readiness and resilience.

A very important part of handling a crisis is the post-calm review process. The recording of emotional status and reason for decision-making after going through the checklist is important to facilitate continual enhancement. This reflection will provoke an investor to ask himself what type of emotions were at work, what choices were made, and whether using the checklist prompted a more level-headed response. The reflective practices above not only improve self-awareness, but they also make up a learning loop, and every crisis would become an opportunity to grow and improve strategies.

Furthermore, practical instrumentation is not limited to an immediate response, but includes self-diagnosis and instantaneous decision-making. An example is the Investor Bias Quiz, which is useful in identifying the psychological triggers involved in investing. Cognitive and emotional biases can be pointed out. On this basis, investors can learn to adjust their approaches to handle those weaknesses, and this directly connects to the practical applications.

Extreme market event scenario playbooks also provide investors with a guide on how to act within the high-stress environment of unexpected market events such as flash crashes or rallies. These playbooks, which are usually visualized as decision trees and flowcharts, give a roadmap of response pathways and include options, including holding, trimming, exiting, or adding positions. Walkthroughs are considered in real-life case studies, which show how such playbooks were used during market episodes.

Finally, crisis management in the financial market is something that boils down to a proactive and all-inclusive course of action. Combining psychological tools, physical grounding, technology support, and rules-based reviews allows the investor to navigate the volatile investment environment of financial crises with a little less fear and a lot more strategic acumen. Such a wide-ranging view protects not only against short-term market shocks but also can give rise to a strong state of mind that can flourish in the waves of volatility that characterize financial markets.

Psychological Resilience in Downturns

In this dynamic sphere of financial markets, psychological resilience proves to be a vital characteristic of investors keen to weather the storms of downturns in a composed and tactically shrewd manner. The common factor here, though, is not just resilience to financial losses but rather resilience to adapt to this, recover, and even grow through this. These features of strength are buttressed by emotional intelligence, cognitive flexibility, and the capability to have a long-term outlook and view short-term failures.

Financial crashes always induce a spiraling effect that may rationalize judgment and result in the uncontrolled processing of decisions. When in such situations, the instinctive reaction and feeling of fear and uncertainty in the human brain may increase the levels of stress, creating a condition known as the fight or flight response. The occurrence of this physiological response is described by increased adrenaline, a loss of peripheral vision, and a tendency to focus on the nearest danger instead of dealing with the situation strategically. Psychologically strong investors are able to become aware of these emotional outlooks and develop methods to reduce them.

Cognitive reframing is one of the aspects of instilling resilience. This is done deliberately by changing the way a person thinks so that the occurrence of a downturn is not seen as world-ending but as a temporary dip or, rather, a growth opportunity. In this regard, historical data can be used as a strong instrument in the sense that it gives support that a market downturn is part of natural financial cycles and that a downturn period can be succeeded by a period of recovery and growth. Restructuring the story will help investors become less anxious and be able to look towards the long-term objectives of their investment.

The second aspect of psychological resilience is the establishment of a well-organised routine comprising aspects such as checking in on emotions and reflection regularly. Such habits can enable the investors to have a stable emotional state so as to avoid the irrational thoughts of panic. Self-awareness and emotional control can be facilitated with the help of techniques like mindfulness meditation, journaling, and visualization exercises. Such habits help investors take a breather, evaluate their emotional disposition, and choose to make rational decisions as opposed to making irrational decisions.

Additionally, resilience is enhanced by the development of a supporting network. Having access to a community of peers, mentors, or accountability partners can help offer powerful perspectives and emotional support when it is hard. Communication of experiences and strategies to a fellow person not only diminishes the feeling of isolation but also the collaborative spirit in solving problems. Such a network may serve as a sort of cushion against the emotional burden of market fluctuations and offer a feeling of stability and common cause.

Also, the practice of a diversified investment portfolio may be a viable risk management strategy and resilience. Diversifying or reducing investments or exposures to a single source of risk by investing in different asset types, across different sectors and geographies. This kind of diversification does more than preclude losses; it can also act as a psychological safety net, since the shock of destabilizing turns becomes a smaller element as it exists as a part of a larger, balanced picture.

Lastly, resilient investors have the capacity to learn from experiences and apply them in future schemes. Post-mortems of successful and unsuccessful investments can be performed to find the cognitive biases and emotional patterns behind decisions that could have affected their success or failure. This observation has given investors the realization to work on these aspects in the hope of further improving their outcomes in future crises.

Conclusively, psychological resilience in financial recession is a complex entity, which is a synergy of emotional intelligence, strategic foresight, and adaptive learning. With the development of these aspects, investors will not only be able to endure the tension of market fluctuation, but they will also be better able to navigate the intricacy of the financial world.

Learning from Crisis Experiences

Living in times of financial crisis provides us with priceless experiences as to what is needed in terms of psychological strength in the face of the financial markets. Such turbulent times bring out the test of investors and compel them to challenge their biases, emotional reactions, and decision-making models. Through investigation of past crises, investors are able to develop a better appreciation of what triggers their psychology as well as what can be done to help counteract the psychological effects of the future financial upheavals that they will face.

Fear and uncertainty are the stimuli during a financial crisis. Such a visceral reaction may give way to panic selling, irrational decisions, and the discontinuation of long-term plans. It is important to know the underlying reasons behind such reactions, which are psychological in nature. Investors usually feel very anxious, and this could make matters worse since emotions can cloud the situation. Being aware of these emotional reactions enables the investors to engage in action plans like mindfulness and emotional regulation to achieve clarity and composure.

Indeed, when considering previous crises, e.g., the financial meltdown of 2008, or the immediate market plunge at the onset of the COVID-19 pandemic, it is possible to draw some general conclusions about the ways in which investors may act. These are over-testing of the short-term movements, caving in to the herd behavior, and failure to follow the set rules in managing risks. By analyzing these behaviours, investors can recognize the cognitive biases that contribute to poor decision-making, including loss aversion, overconfidence, and recency bias.

These experiences do not only require learning through identification of mistakes but also through the ability to establish positive changes in order to avoid them in the future. This method has to be done with some ongoing training and self-exposure. To help manage any stress or fear that may overcome them during a time of volatility, investors can also consider creating a crisis playbook, i.e., a set of personal rules that may specify specific actions to follow in a period of market volatility. This playbook must contain emotional checks, risk evaluation, and decision-making procedures that are more demanding on long-term goals than emotion-driven short-term responses.

In addition, growth entails undertaking a post-crisis review. After every market downturn, investors are advised to carry out a debrief to see what was successful and what did not work and why. This introspection can assist in combating the sins of the past and turning them into positive learning experiences, and the brain is a process of constant upgrading. Moreover, such insights could also be shared with a peer group in the form of mentorship to continue learning and obtain a different perspective on how to cope with the future crisis.

Applying the lessons of a crisis event to day-to-day investment procedures could result in the creation of behavioral alpha--a competitive advantage achieved through emotional control and the art of psychological alacrity. It includes such habits as developing resilient attitudes through frequent self-examination, a healthy emotional balance, and consistently sound risk management plans. Internalization of these practices will enable investors to mitigate the uncertainties that are bound to occur in the financial markets.

Finally, the capability to inform oneself after the experience of crises is the primary feature of a successful investor. It demands an active attitude towards cognition of the personal responses that characterize the psyche, receptiveness towards the modification, and the ability to keep the rule of transferring the knowledge to further ordeals. In so doing, investors not only increase their financial savvy but also develop the emotional strength that is required to perform well in the constantly changing environment of financial markets.

Chapter 14: Conclusion and Path Forward

Summarizing Key Insights

Financial markets represent a complicated maze of interwoven human behaviour and patterns. In such a complex environment, a grasp of the outermost barely noticeable but unerringly strong psychological undercurrents is of utmost importance to any investor who seeks to ride the choppy waters of market forces. It is this delve into the psychological perspective of the financial markets that can demonstrate that the ability to unleash the powers of the mind can be a great influence over investment decisions.

At the outset, the process starts with the acknowledgement of hidden psychological forces that influence investment decisions in subtle ways. These forces may go undetected, but they can hold a lot of power over the decisions of an investor. Examples include cognitive biases, or mental traps to which even the most intelligent investors succumb, making them make mistakes in judgment and decision-making. It is very important to identify and deactivate such prejudices. Besides, there is an overconfidence bias when investors are overconfident in their opinions and might underestimate the risks, thus making irrational decisions, especially in bull markets.

The other important lesson is how the operations of emotional regulation retain the resiliency of the market. Successful investors control emotions in volatile market conditions, unlike the rest. Emotional control is the process of reigning in fear, greed, and panic, which may cloud judgment when the market is high or low. Learning to take a step back and reassess at such emotional peaks is the key to the rational course of investing.

Besides, the book identifies the significance of useful decision-making tools that incorporate psychological acumen. These tools enable the investors to employ strategies that are not only data-driven alone, but also that are behaviorally aware. Quantitative analysis, by trying to counter-balance it with qualitative insights or calibrated intuition in decision-making frameworks, is highlighted as it can guide an investor in resolving uncertainty using a more holistic approach.

The financial markets are also large contributors to group psychology. Groupthink's resulting dynamics may create a trap of consensus because minority opinion is blocked, thus increasing risk. By getting a sense of such dynamics, as well as by encouraging authentic dissent in the right environment, one can avoid otherwise very expensive herd-driven mistakes.

The book uses pointing out lessons about the practical application of psychological agility to give a competitive advantage in current cases. The possibility to be flexible and learn based on old experience, but be open to new knowledge, is essential. Investors are also urged to adopt lifestyles that influence them to develop a self-evaluation and reflection on the self-requirement, ensuring they never stop improving and recovering after market cycles.

Lastly, the text firmly notes the power of self-awareness and disciplined patterns in driving behaviour to enhance behavioral alpha. It encompasses extra income realized due to psychological training, which is rather higher than the benefits accrued by technical mastery. The psychological insight in the context of investment strategies will help investors build a strong edge, which would hold across time.

To sum up, the synthesis of psychological understanding into the tissue of investment not only stimulates better decision-making but also helps investors change failures into a source of improvement. With the right mentality of constant learning and adapting, investors will be able to create a sustainable roadmap on their journey towards long-term wealth generation through their navigation in the financial markets with an essence of confidence and clarity.

Implementing Psychological Strategies

Financial markets are a complex environment, where the presence of analytical acumen does not always translate into success; rather, it can be said that investment success can also rely on the respective psychology of investors. The use of psychological methods entails a careful fusion of emotions, thoughtfulness, and action modification. It helps investors to ride the turbulent seas of the market with more grace and effectiveness.

Developing emotional intelligence should be regarded as one of the key elements of applying psychological strategies. Emotions in the roaring world of financial trading may be a powerful asset and formidable enemy. Investors should form a highly developed sense of personal emotional conditions and causes of emotional reactions, where they should be able to recognize and deal with their emotions of fear, greed, and anxiety. Mindfulness and reflective journaling techniques are an invaluable ally in this endeavour as they help one gain a more thorough comprehension of emotional responses and allow one to be a more informed decision-maker. Emotional stability serves to keep the investor out of reckless moves caused by the vagaries of the moment.

The other important element is the detection and reduction of cognitive biases. The brain of a human being is merely programmed to find patterns and shortcuts, which brings intolerance, bigotry, and prejudice that may distort judgment and decision-making. Other typical biases in financial markets are overconfidence, anchoring, and confirmation bias. The measures to address these biases are focused on purposeful adherence to challenge the assumptions, form different views, and think critically. These distortions can be addressed by routinely taking stock of such distortions through investment decision audit practice, where investors systematically examine their decision-making process and correct them to lead to more rational and objective investment decisions.

In addition, the formulation of individual personal decision frameworks must be applied to work out effective psychological approaches. These frameworks are systematic sets of rules that establish certain rules pertaining to entry and exit trades, risk management, and market perception. Following these pre-determined strategies, investors would be in a better position to curb the effect of emotional and cognitive distortions when making decisions that align with their long-term investment plans. Pre-trade checklists and scenario-based playbooks can be especially effective in keeping you on the path of disciplined decision-making as a physical reference to guide you when the market is at its most volatile.

Accountability and Peer support are also important in the effective application of psychological strategies. Being able to talk to other investors in a similar position enables the exchange of information and experience, as well as feedback, to strive towards a culture of constant learning and advancing. Through accountability groups, investors are able to discuss their struggles and achievements, and get positive feedback and support. This form of collaboration, in addition to personal resilience, adds up to the outlook in market dimension, as well as the concept of how a market behaves under the influence of behavioral factors.

Psychological strategies used in financial markets, in essence, are a complex process that involves taking an oath to the cause and self-improvement and discipline. By incorporating the implementation of emotional intelligence, cognitive awareness, and rigid decision-making models, investors can increase their aptitude in navigating the multifaceted nature of the market and eventually succeed and stabilize in their venture investor pursuits.

Commitment to Lifelong Learning

Financial markets are an ever-changing place where knowledge is a lifelong learning activity, which needs discipline and flexibility. The financial markets are a dynamic environment with fast-changing trends in technology and regulation, and the ability to maintain the shifting economic environment. In this regard, constant practice of learning and adaptation is not just a useful quality, but it is really a necessary one that someone aiming at excelling in this sphere must have.

Among the main factors of committing oneself to lifelong learning is the need to realize that the knowledge and skills that were successful in the past will not be enough to tackle future needs. This demands an open mind that is ready to change and accepts new approaches and attitudes. In an attempt to survive the competitive market, investors and financial professionals are to be actively involved in the search for new sources of information and insights that are capable of providing a better understanding of the market dynamics.

Coupling the mix of educational platforms is a viable way of ensuring that you stay ahead in the financial markets. That involves purchases of industry publications, seminars, workshops, and online classes. Not only do such activities enable the acquisition of good knowledge, but they also allow interacting with colleagues and specialists and sharing ideas and best practices.

Besides, the necessity to learn from past experiences cannot be overestimated. Analyzing past victories and losses will enable people to get insights into how they make their judgments and what can be done to enhance them. This type of reflection is essential to the process of gaining more insight into personal weaknesses and strengths and, as a result, producing better-informed and more strategic decision-making.

Besides educating at school and self-reflection, mentorship is also a major aspect of lifelong learning. It is priceless to have a mentor who can give guidance, feedback, and support. Mentors have the advantage of hindsight, can advise on tricky circumstances, and can offer points of view that are not immediately obvious. A mentor-mentee relationship creates a learning culture of learning and developing.

In addition, accepting technology changes is another major element of continuing learning in the financial industry. Technology is transforming the financial marketplace, and the users who utilize the tools have a lot to benefit from. Regardless of whether advanced analytics, artificial intelligence, or the blockchain becomes the universal truth, when it comes to the better identification of investment decisions and maximization of operational efficiencies, staying on top of technological trends is a necessity.

Lastly, a determination to lifelong learning is based on the importance of formulating a curious attitude. This entails being willing to examine revolutionary ideas, ask questions, and counter assumptions. Innovation and creativity are important factors in discovering new opportunities and being ahead of the trends, and curiosity prompts people.

To sum up, the lifelong learning commitment is a strategic necessity of the financial markets. It demands a proactive style of teaching, thinking, guidance, and embracing new technologies. With such a culture of lifelong learning, people can become capable of adapting to any changes and become successful over time in the non-stationary world of finance.

Future Trends in Market Psychology

The financial environment in the world is exponentially dynamic, so it is a matter of concern to know what to expect in terms of market psychology in the future. The psychological dimension of investments changes with the markets that are still affected by technological breakthroughs, social processes, and macro trends, thus requiring a subtle understanding of changes.

The emerging digital investment platforms and democratization of trading are among the most important trends that will happen in the future of market psychology. The expansion of online trading through application and Service platforms has driven the trading to the bottom end of the market, allowing a new and younger type of investor, often with strong ties to social media as a source of information and potential signals to leverage. This change has increased the power of density of collective behaviour, in which any trends and sentiments may be disseminated very quickly throughout digital communities. One example of the market is the emergence of meme stocks and the boom in cryptocurrencies, which demonstrates that the dynamic of the market could be influenced by digital communication; frequently, the financial indicators are irrelevant.

On top of that, market psychology becomes all the more complex now that artificial intelligence and machine learning are gaining a greater presence in the trading sphere. Algorithms have also significantly affected the decision-making processes by starting to analyze large quantities of data at a much faster speed than humans could perform. Nevertheless, the dependence on technology may also be related to overconfidence in algorithms' predictions, which may increase market volatility where models with inconsiderable variability or black swans are not considered.

The psychological effect of such technologies is immense since they make investors feel safe without a foundation. Having said that, the infallibility of technological tools can be associated with riskier behavior because investors can fail to understand that human judgment and emotional intelligence play a significant role in making decisions. In general, as a corrective measure, in the market, psychology of the future may inculcate a fair measure of emotional and conscious Education to balance the use of the technological instruments and end up investors with a critical mind.

Moreover, the increasing understanding of behavioral finance will determine an upsurge in market psychology in the future. Investors are becoming more aware of mental mistakes and feelings and thoughts that affect how they trade. The need for educational materials and tools that teach self-awareness and emotional control grows accordingly. It is probably due to this trend that more advanced training programs and materials could be developed to foster a rigorously robust investment psychology.

Parallel with these developments in education, more personalization of financial guidance and tools will be used in the future based on a psychological profile. The trend is connected to an overall movement toward recognizing that each investor has different psychological profiles, and using data-informed intuition to provide personalized solutions that accommodate the investor based on their risk threshold, behavioral biases, and emotionally driven tendencies.

Moreover, the role of global events in the psychology of the market is underestimated. With geopolitical tensions, climate change, and pandemics still representing a massive threat in terms of uncertainty, investors will most likely turn more sensitive to the psychological effects that these events have. The awareness can result in a greater emphasis on scenario planning and stress testing in investment planning, as investors attempt to make their way in the complexity of a fast-changing world.

On the whole, combining technology with behavioral knowledge and individual plans will remain a trend in market psychology in the future. As sophisticated applications are developed further and become available to a greater number of investors, it will be up to psychological acumen to take on the challenges of the day in the world of the modern financial markets and be versatile and resilient to deal with change. In the wake of such trends, the capacity to learn and leverage market psychology will become the determinant of long-term success in investment.

EPILOGUE

As we draw the curtain on this exploration of psychology within the financial markets, it's essential to reflect on the profound insights gained and the tools acquired. Throughout this journey, we have delved into the invisible forces that shape our investment decisions, unraveling the complexities of cognitive biases and emotional dynamics that often go unnoticed but wield substantial influence over our financial outcomes.

The essence of mastering the mental game of investing lies not in the eradication of emotions, but in the conscious regulation and understanding of them. By recognizing our biases, whether it be the allure of recency bias or the pitfalls of herd mentality, we equip ourselves with the ability to make more informed and rational decisions. This awareness transforms potential vulnerabilities into strengths, creating a foundation for sustainable growth and resilience.

The narratives shared, from the lessons of past market manias to the strategic frameworks for emotional regulation, serve as both a mirror and a guide. They reflect the shared experiences of countless investors who have navigated the tumultuous seas of the financial markets, learning to cultivate calm amidst chaos and to harness fear as a tool for insight rather than a trigger for impulsive action.

The call to action is clear: embrace continuous learning and self-assessment as cornerstones of your investment strategy. By integrating checklists, playbooks, and behavioral dashboards into your routine, you create a personalized system that not only tracks financial performance but also monitors mental and emotional health. This holistic approach ensures that decisions are not only data-driven but also emotionally intelligent.

In an era where information is abundant and market conditions are perpetually evolving, the ability to adapt and remain psychologically agile is paramount. As markets shift and new challenges arise, the tools and strategies discussed in these pages will serve as a compass, guiding you through uncertainty with confidence and clarity.

Every investor has the potential to transform setbacks into wisdom and uncertainty into opportunity. By fostering a mindset that prioritizes psychological resilience and decision-making mastery, you position yourself not just to survive the markets but to thrive within them. Let this be the beginning of a lifelong commitment to mastering the mental aspects of investing, transforming your approach to risk, and accumulating long-term wealth with assurance and poise.

www.ingramcontent.com/pod-product-compliance
Lightning Source LLC
Chambersburg PA
CBHW060506280326
41933CB00014B/2883